The Complete Third Down Manual

The 2016 New Orleans Saints

Robert J Peters

Richard Kusisto

TABLE OF CONTENTS

Robert J Peters & Richard Kusisto II

Introduction

After watching countless hours of NFL game film (yes, it is an addiction), I often find myself focusing on third down situational play calling. Games are often won or lost on decisions made on third down. It's the money down, convert to stay on the field, or fail and punt.

In general, success on first and second down are all about execution. Teams will call their base run plays and play action concepts to move the ball and stay out of third downs all together. Once in a while teams will take chances on early downs, but this is not the norm throughout a game.

Third downs typically involve more game planning, and are often drop back pass situations (unless it is third and short). Defensive coordinators will often save their best blitzes for these situations as well.

Looking at statistics from the 2016 NFL season, the New Orleans Saints had a league best 48.6% conversion percentage on third down. They also converted 13/15 of their fourth downs, finishing second in this category behind Dallas.

This introduction contains a summary of a quick statistical breakdown for the entire season. Each succeeding chapter will diagram each individual play, and the defense's response.

Concept Efficiency

Concept	Times Called	First Down %
PA 3 man flat*	3	100%
H Post**	6	83%
Double Moves	4	75%
Dive	21	67%
Toss	6	67%
Stick	9	67%
3 Man Drive	8	63%
Four Verticals	11	55%
Spade	15	53%
10 Yard Out	6	50%
Middle Read Y Cross	11	45%
Hank	10	40%
2 Man Drive	11	36%
Wheel	7	14%

*PA 3 man flat (Pages 66 & 98): This play was a go – to call on fourth downs, as well as two point conversions. The Saints reserved a few key third downs in the red zone for it as well. It is a high percentage, safe concept that gives the quarterback a flurry of quick options, while using misdirection to get defenders out of place. The concept floods the play side flat with three receivers, all spaced accordingly.

**H Post (Pages 24, 52, 96, 114, 156): This concept features an option route as the primary read, with auxiliary routes to replace defenders if the defense wants to double team the option route. This play has its own chapter in "The Melting Pot", and how to adapt it to high school and college offenses. You can find this book on Amazon.

3rd & 1-2

1-2 Yards Needed	
Total	58
Conversion %	71%
Run	53%
Pass	47%
Most common call #1	Dive (FB or TB)
Most common call #2	Toss (TB flip or regular)
Most common call #3	Slants

3rd & 3-5

3-5 Yards Needed	
Total	54
Conversion %	61%
Run	13%
Pass	87%
Most common call #1	Slot Fade*
Most common call #2	3 Man Drive**
Most common call #3	Middle Read***

*Slot Fade (Pages 196, 254): This play epitomizes the attacking nature of the Saints offense. The purpose of the play is to create a one on one matchup with the slot receiver, on a fade route. The tight split from the slot gives him extra room to create the outside leverage and vertical separation he needs. Often times a linebacker or larger box safety will match up with the receiver in the slot, a matchup that will favor the offense. The concept works well against zone as well, with a hitch route on the outside to keep the corner occupied.

**3 Man Drive (Page 388): (see next page for description)

***Middle Read (Pages 70, 88, 232, 354): This concept will give the quarterback one on one matchups, incorporating the slot fades explained above. If the defense brackets the fades, the deep cross and underneath routes will space the remaining defenders out to take advantage of the open space.

3ʳᵈ & 6-10

6-10 Yards Needed	
Total	71
Conversion %	35%
Run	3%
Pass	97%
Most common call #1	2 Man Drive*
Most common call #2	Four Verticals
Most common call #3	Middle Read/Y Cross

*2 Man Drive (Pages 158, 446): The Saints use the drive concept on third downs quite often. Their two man drive will use different frontside combinations, depending on their opponent. The quarterback will read the front side first. If these routes are covered, the drag and dig will enter his vision. A running back check down will often be the last read on these plays.

3ʳᵈ & 10 +

10+ Yards Needed	
Total	29
Conversion %	28%
Run	12%
Pass	90%
Most common call #1	Some type of screen
Most common call #2	Four verticals
Most common call #3	Hank*

*Hank (Page 74): Hank is a whole field curl flat concept. The curl flat pattern is mirrored on both sides, with a receiver running a spot route over the middle to occupy the inside linebackers.

Week 1 vs Oakland

3ʳᵈ &10   Ball on own 25   1ˢᵗ Quarter 14:52

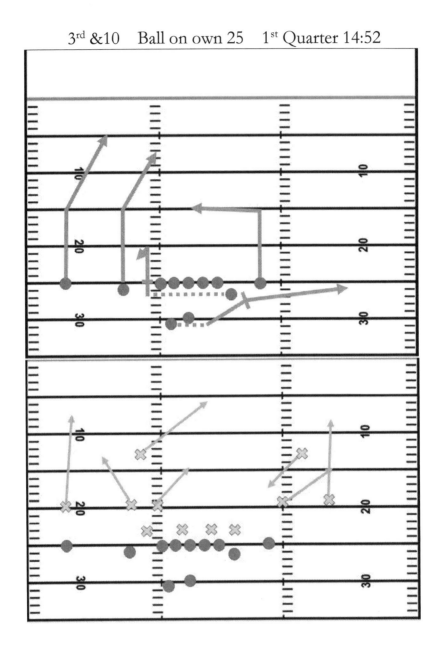

Progression Read:

1. Inside Post
2. Outside Post
3. TE Chip – Release Sit route
4. Dig
5. Chip – Release Flat Route

The Saints give their quarterback a full field progression read on their first third down of the season. The double post concept is meant to take advantage of an aggressive cover 3 or cover 4.

The Raiders call a base cover three. They buzz the weak safety down to defend the weak hook zone, while rushing the four down lineman.

With the free safety playing closer to the double post combination, there isn't much room to fit the ball in. Brees resets his feet to find the dig route, which is guarded by the weak safety rolling down.

Pressure gets to the quarterback, which causes a sack and brings up a fourth down.

3rd & 1   Ball on own 20   1st Quarter 11:59

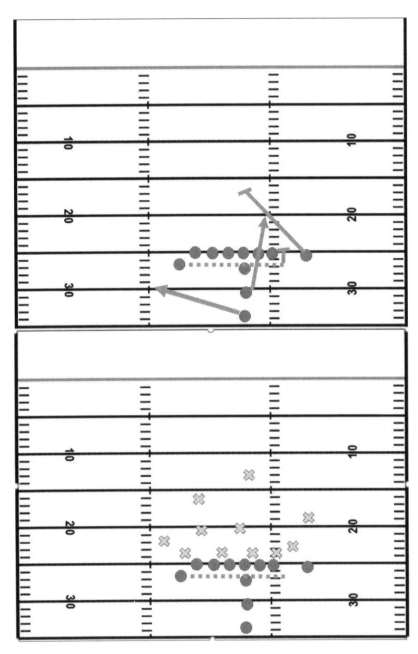

On their first third and short, the Saints call a quick – hitting fullback dive. The key to this play is the double team from the center and right guard on the one technique. If the offense can get some push here, they should easily pick up the one yard needed for a first down.

The Raiders bring their inside linebackers hard, but when the offense only needs one yard, it is nearly impossible to come hard enough.

The Saints get a solid push, and pick up about two yards and a first down.

3ʳᵈ & 8 Ball on Raiders 18 1ˢᵗ Quarter 6:56

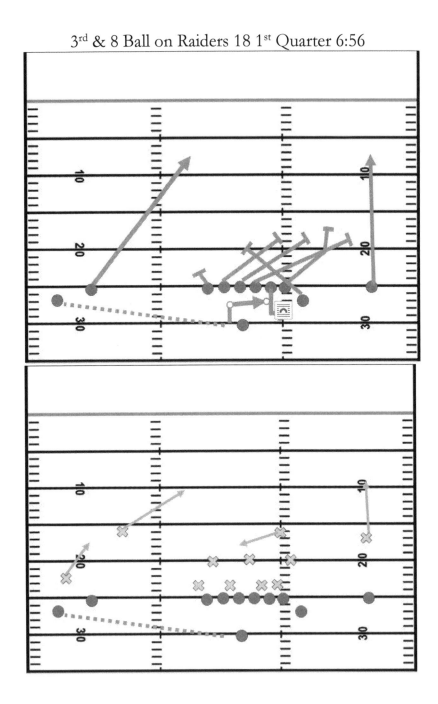

The Saints are faced with a 3rd and 8 at the Oakland 11 yard line. With points pretty much on the board New Orleans does not want to do anything to take themselves out of that position.

Initially the Saints line up in empty with the RB split far out to the left. They motion him in to the left of Brees with not much change in the defense which means they are most likely in some sort of zone coverage. The Saints choose to run a screen here, a conservative call to ensure they stay in field goal range.

Since Oakland is in a zone, they are able to sniff out the screen and the RB ends up getting tackled right at the line of scrimmage, forcing Brees to just throw the ball in the turf, which brings up a Saints field goal attempt.

3rd & 1   Ball on own 34   1st Quarter 0:48

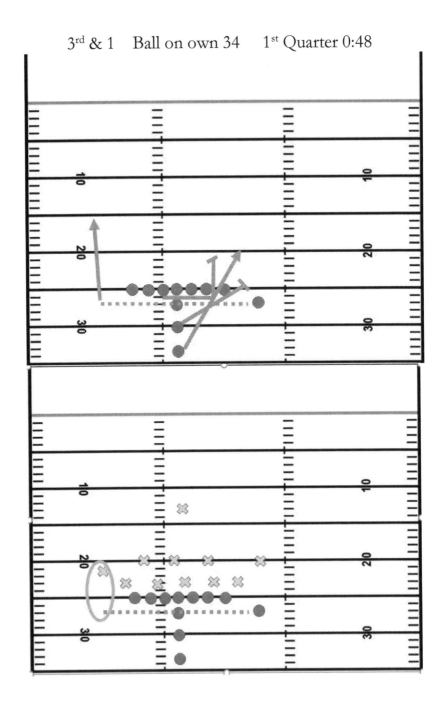

Faced with another 3rd and short New Orleans sends out its 22 big personnel once again. A common theme for the Saints is to get set on offense, wait for the defense to set up then motion someone across the formation to see how the defense reacts to get some sort of an idea of what the defense has planned.

The Saints run one of the most popular and hardnosed plays in football, Power. Everyone on the play side will block down with a double team on the 5 technique working to the middle linebacker. The FB is able to get a good kick out on the end man on the line of scrimmage and the backside guard pulls through the hole and cuts off the inside backer. The Saints pick up the first down from some nice blocking up front.

3rd & Goal   Ball on Raiders 5   2nd Quarter 12:51

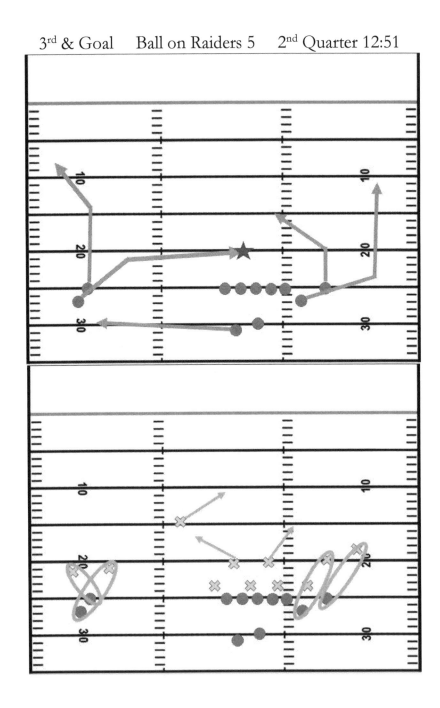

Progression read:

1. Alert: Corner
2. Slant
3. Wheel
4. Drag
5. RB Swing

Faced with a 3rd & medium on their own goal line, the Saints come out with stacked receivers to the left and a wing with a condensed split to the right.

The defense plays man coverage with 2 defenders playing inside/out technique to the stacked receiver side. The corner route doubles as a "pick" route if the defense were to play straight man.

The slant is designed to get quick inside leverage and to make the LB cover the wheel route have to work extremely hard to get out and cover.

The defense ends up defending the play very well, but eventually the drag route comes open. The receiver gets tackled by the hook defender on that side of the field, and brings up fourth down.

3rd & 1   Ball on own 41   2nd Quarter 2:00

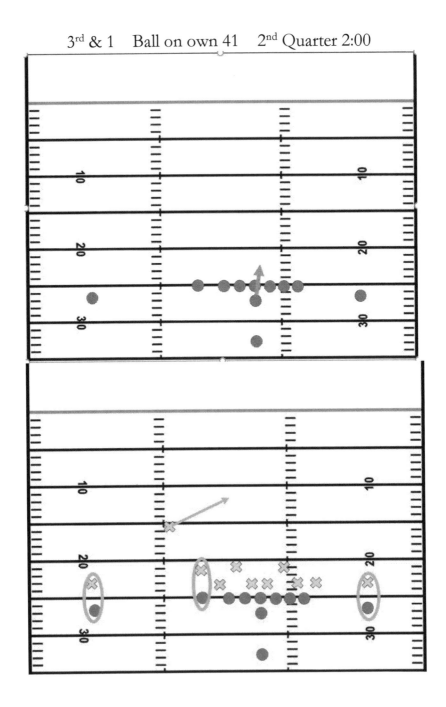

The fast way from point A to point B is a straight line and that Saints what the Saints do here with the QB sneak. The defense lines up with 2 A gap defenders on the line of scrimmage with no one in either B gap giving the offense a 3 on 2 advantage at the point of attack. Saints are able to create enough movement up front to move the pile and get a 1st down.

3rd & 4   Ball on Raiders 48   2nd Quarter 1:26

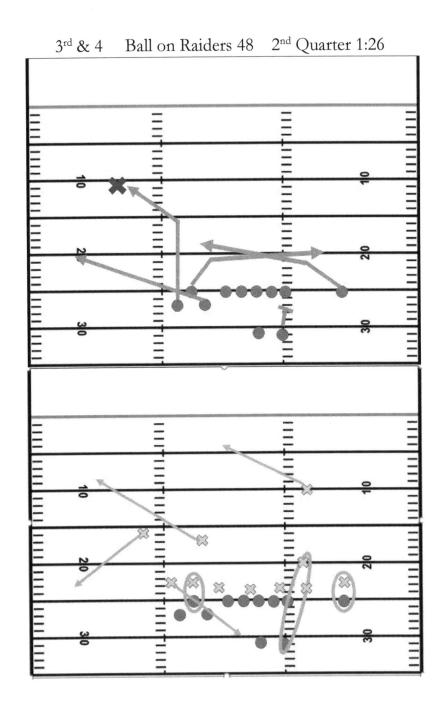

Progression Read:

1. Corner
2. Flat
3. Shallow coming to the left
4. Drag going to the right

New Orleans comes out with a bunch set to the left close to the tackle and the single receiver tight to the formation on the right. The Raiders play the bunch very similar as they did the stack formation earlier. The point man is pressed at the line of scrimmage and is tailed by man coverage. They play inside/out coverage once again. The single receiver is man up also with the FS free to follow the QB's eyes.

Brees takes the snap and sees the CB come down on the flat route which gives the corner route outside leverage on the defender over him. Brees throws the ball to only where his man get it which ends up falling incomplete near the sideline.

3ʳᵈ & 10   Ball on own 10   3ʳᵈ Quarter 12:24

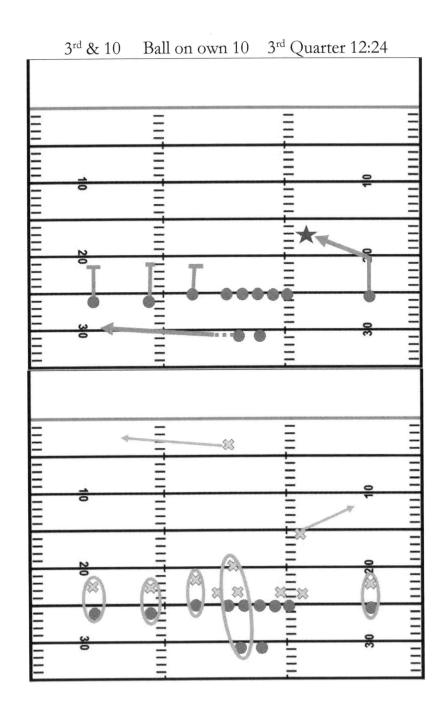

Progression Read
1. Slant
2. Swing

The Saints find themselves in a 3rd & long here and will try to use the defenses' speed against them. With press coverage across the board, it is safe to assume that the defense is in man coverage.

With trips to the left and the running back set to the left also, the Saints quick motion the back out to try and out flank the defense. On the right side of the formation they have the single receiver on a slant route. With this formation, the offense is trying to read the Will LB. The offense will throw opposite of where the Will goes to get a numbers or leverage advantage.

With the defense in man coverage, the Will flies out to cover the RB making the read for Brees crystal clear and he zips the ball into the slant route. Initially the receiver does a great job of getting the CB to turn his hips outside but the CB does a fantastic job of recovering and making the tackle before the first down can be made.

3rd & 4   Ball on Raiders 49   3rd Quarter 0:43

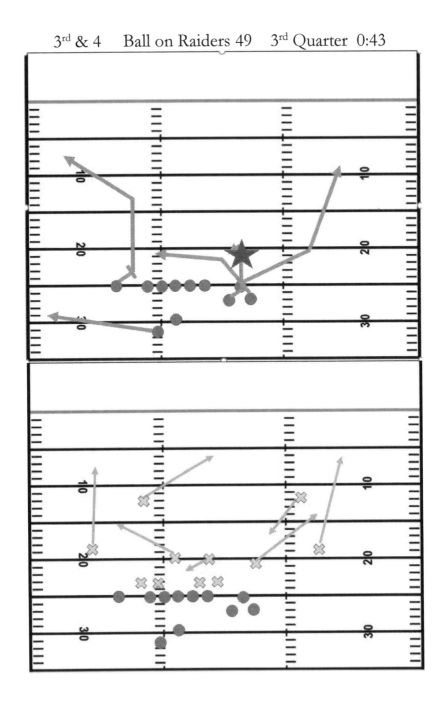

Progression Read:

1. Alert: Wheel
2. Spot Route
3. Drag
4. RB Check Down

The progression on this play follows the classic "H Post" concept used most notably Mike Martz. The Saints appear to be reading the drag before the spot/option route. The play isolates the strong side linebacker or nickel with an option route. The drag route is meant to occupy the inside linebacker, and the wheel route occupies the corner.

The Raiders appear to be playing a "box" call to the three man bunch. The call gives the defense four defenders over three receivers. The defenders will match the first two inside routes, and the first two outside routes.

With the drag route and wheel route occupying the two underneath defenders, the spot route sits in the void between the two. The quarterback hits the receiver on time to pick up a first down.

3rd & 8 Ball on Raiders 33 4th Quarter 14:15

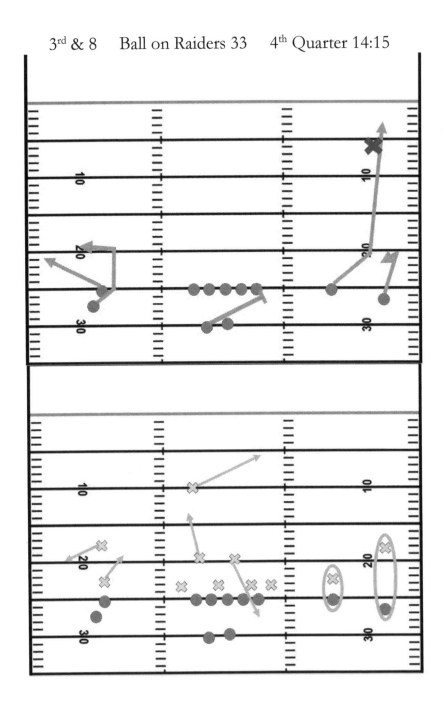

Facing a 3rd & long, the Saints come out in 11 personnel but switch out an RB for a FB. They stack the receivers to the left and flex their TE out to see who matches up with him.

The Raiders play man coverage across the board with inside/out technique to the stack. Matched up with the TE is the strong safety so as Brees takes his drop he decides to take the shot to his big body TE. The ball is underthrown and the safety is able to make a play and tip the ball incomplete.

3ʳᵈ & Goal   Ball on Raiders 6   4ᵗʰ Quarter 9:31

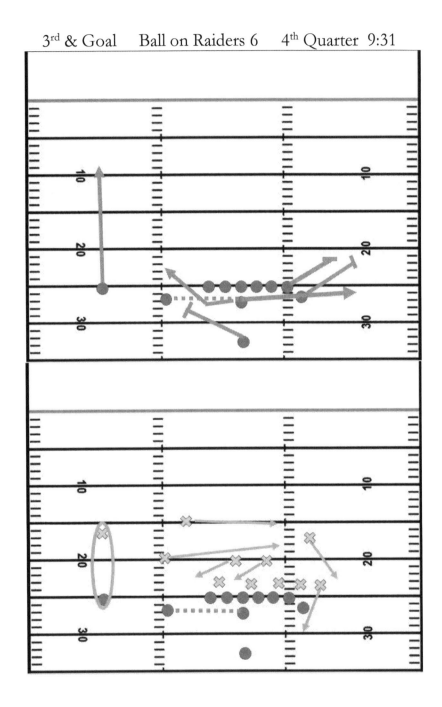

With a 3rd & Goal coming up for the offense, the Saints bring in 12 personnel and set up with a TE and wing to the right and twins to the right. They have given this look before with motioning the slot over to fake the jet sweep and hand off the ball the other way. This time the Saints show a different wrinkle.

When the slot gets sent into motion both the man across from him and the free safety take off in his direction. Brees takes the snap, quick fakes to the jet motion then takes it himself around the left side of the formation. It looks like the running back was a lead blocker but he was set so far back that he doesn't have an opportunity to get out in front of Brees. The tackle is made before he can get into the end zone.

Week 2 at Giants

3rd & 5   Ball on own 43   1st Quarter 13:04

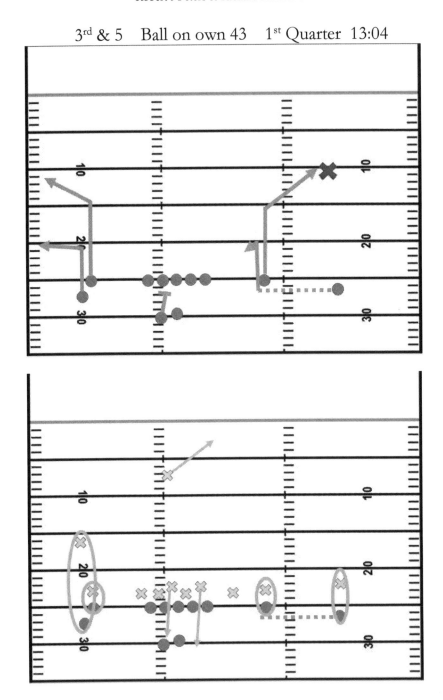

Facing their first 3rd down of the game the Saints come out with stacked receivers to the left and doubles to the right with a flexed out TE. The Giants show man coverage across the board with everyone within a few yards from the line of scrimmage other than the FS. Brees suspects a blitz to be coming so he keeps the back in for protection.

Brees appears to be targeting the motion man on the right side. There appears to be some indecision on the break point of the route, as the receiver hesitates to run the hitch route. Brees resets his eyes to the corner route, and decides to throw there.

The ball falls incomplete to the turf with the stop route wide open and perhaps a first down opportunity lost.

3rd & 9   Ball on own 33   1st Quarter 10:19

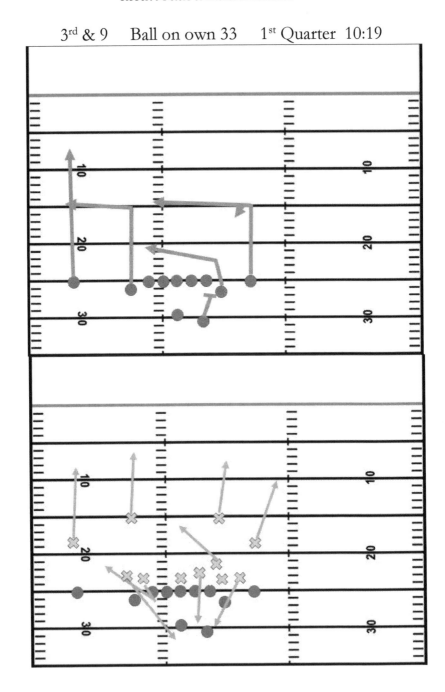

Progression Read

    1.Fade
    2. 10 Yard out
    3. Shallow route
    4. Dig

The protection appears to be called to the wrong side on this play. The center slides to the same side the back is helping on, which leaves three rushers on two guys to the offense's left

The Giants do bring pressure with the 2 outside defenders on the line of scrimmage and the Mike linebacker. The defensive end on the left initially rushes, which occupies the left tackle. He then drops into a pass coverage, which allows the linebacker to rush freely at the quarterback

Brees takes the snap, comes off his first read, hitch steps and just as he is about to throw the ball to the wide open out route, the rush from the left side gets to him and he is forced to tuck the ball and take a sack.

3rd & 3   Ball on own 10   1st Quarter 1:55

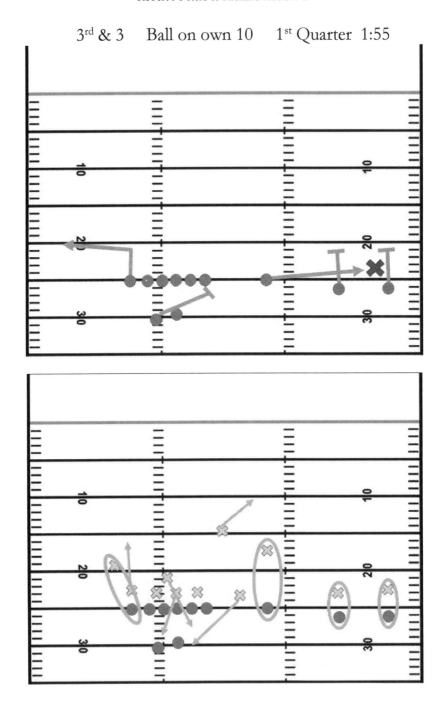

With a 3rd and short opportunity in front of them, the Saints come out in trips to the right with a stand up TE to the left. Once again, the Giants show man coverage and bring pressure with the outside backer to the right and with a X stunt between the Nose tackle and the Mike backer.

The 2 previous 3rd downs the Giants brought pressure and it affected the throw. This time the Saints call a great play to combat the pressure and get the ball out quick to the perimeter and their athletes into space. The 2 outside receivers run interference routes or what most defensive coaches would call "picks".

The Saints get a perfect look with the guy over the inside slot playing 5 yards off. Brees catches the snap and throws the ball to the wide open flat runner but the ball is high and behind and it falls to the turf incomplete.

3rd & 10 Ball on 50 2nd Quarter 12:46

Progression Read:

1. Fade
2. 10 Yard Out
3. Dig
4. TE option route

To this point in the game the Saints have not been able to convert a 3rd down. New York has been able to pressure Brees, make him uncomfortable in the pocket, and this third down is no different.

The Giants game plan is crystal clear: bring blitzers to the side on the tight end. The Saints like to use their tight ends to chip defensive ends on their way out to being check down receivers. The Giants know this, and see it as an opportunity to blitz. By the time Brees gets to his tight ends (typically the third our fourth read), he will have an unblocked defender in his face. The blitz will not be hurt by a hot route, as the tight end will be delaying his release.

Brees goes through his progression with his first 3 options blanketed with coverage. Brees then resets his feet to hit the backside TE option route. The RB is confused, as he has two unblocked guys to pick up. Brees is taken to the ground for another 3rd down sack.

3rd & 4   Ball on own 35   2nd Quarter 7:41

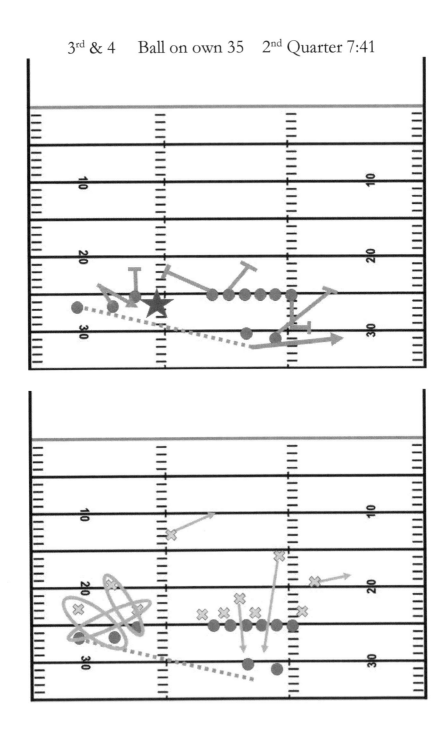

Facing a 3rd and medium, the Saints get creative and use a misdirection slot tunnel screen. They use "orbit" motion to move the defense out of position to get leverage for the blocks.

When the Saints send the man in motion, they get the inside defender to the trips to run with him leaving a 2 on 2 to the quick screen side. With a two man bunch, teams will typically press one, and play off coverage on the second. With the man playing 5 yards off the outside receiver, Brees likes this match up and decides to take it.

The corner makes a heads up play, recognizing the screen immediately and blows up the play for yet another failed 3rd down for the Saints.

3rd & 15 Ball on Giants 30 Quarter 2 3:40

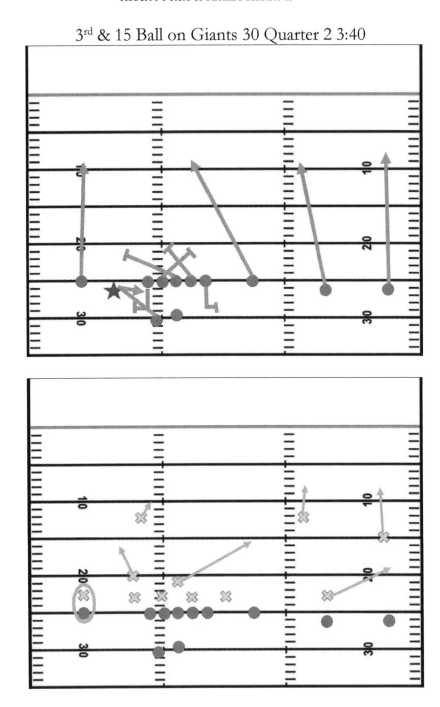

The Saints find themselves in a 3rd and long situation after an offensive pass interference call earlier in the drive. They call a delayed screen to their running back.

Saints come out in a trips formation, with their tight end flexed out wide. The Giants man up to single receiver side with the safety over the top and play a Cover 4 to the field side. The Saints get a favorable look here at the snap, the middle linebacker works to wall off the seam route by the TE and the middle is left wide open.

Luckily for the Giants, the strong safety to the boundary comes up and makes a solid tackle to leave the ball carrier just short of the first down. To this point in the game, the Saints have no answers on 3rd down. They have failed to convert on their first six attempts.

3rd & 9   Ball on own 26   2nd Quarter 1:56

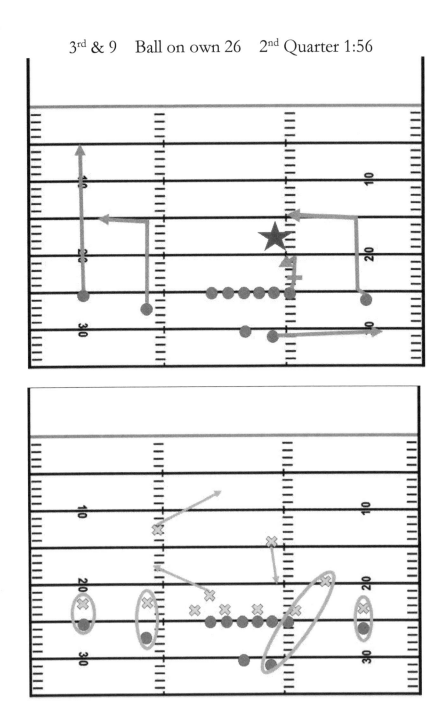

Progression Read:

1. Fade
2. 10 yard out
3. Dig
4. TE chip release spot
5. RB swing

The Saints find themselves in a 3rd and long as time winds down in the half. They come out in a 2x2 set with the Giants showing press coverage once again. The Giants end up playing Cover 1 but they have the boundary safety rob while the field safety drops to the deep middle.

The defender over the slot on the left plays with outside leverage. This forces the quarterback to look elsewhere, despite the one on one matchup.

Brees resents his feet, and hits the dig route in rhythm to pick up a first down during this two minute drill.

3rd & 1   Ball on Giants 25   2nd Quarter :45

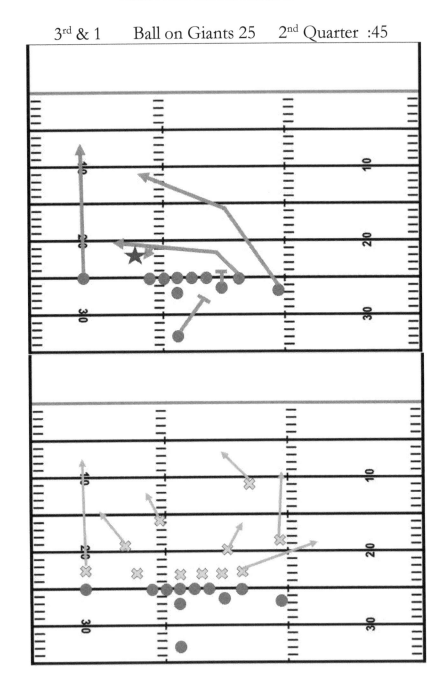

Progression Read:

1. Fade
2. Shallow
3. Deep cross

The Saints find themselves in a 3rd and short and decide condense their formation with a bunch alignment to the right and a single receiver to the left. The Giants initially show press at the line but then spot drop to pass coverage while only rushing 4.

Brees flash fakes the RB to the right and sets up in the pocket. He takes a quick glance at the fade then comes down to his second read on the shallow route as the WR settles in the void. Brees dumps the ball down to him and he gets enough for the first down.

3rd & 18   Ball on Giants 28   2nd Quarter 0:15

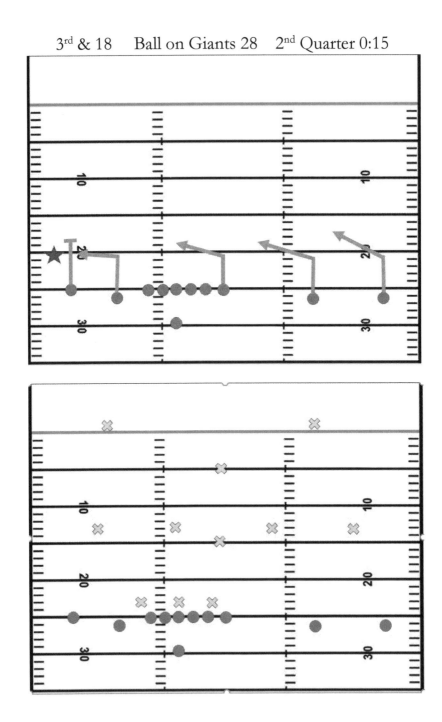

With time almost out in the first half, the Saints have one last play before they have to settle for a field goal. Saints come out in an empty look with the RB in the slot to the left and a TE and 2 WR to the right. The Giants are well aware of the situation and come out in a prevent defense.

The Saints run a quick screen to the left with the outside receiver blocking and all slants backside. Brees dumps the ball off to his RB to let him make a move in space. While this is another "failed" third down attempt, there was never any real effort to convert it. New Orleans was just trying to help itself out and set up a closer field goal attempt.

3rd & 7   Ball on Giants 43   3rd Quarter 9:40

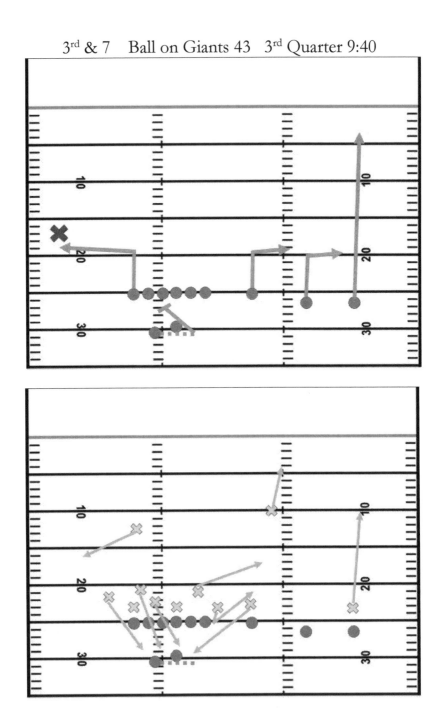

Coverage Read:

1. Hit stick concept on the right if defense gives you leverage.
2. Vs man: look to TE on boundary out

The Saints come out with trips to the field and a stand up TE to the boundary. The last few 3rd downs the Giants did not bring much pressure and ended up giving up a few 1st downs. The Giants pick up on this tendency, and bring pressure. The Giants come back with a boundary pressure and drop the DE to the field into coverage.

The defense shows pre-snap that the offense will have leverage to the wide side of the field. The stick concept is open. Brees senses the pressure and moves the RB to the other side of him, perhaps get him out of the throwing lane to his TE on the out route. The boundary safety has no worries about the big TE beating him deep and sits on the out route. Brees' throw is high and outside and falls to the turf incomplete.

3rd & 7   Ball on own 29   3rd Quarter 2:20

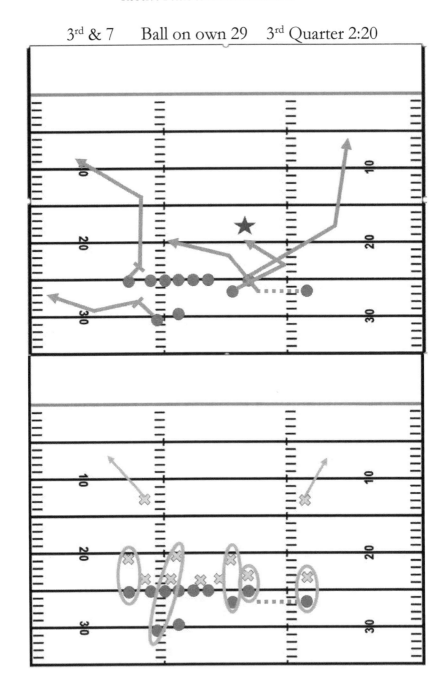

Progression Read:

1. Pre-snap peek Wheel Route
2. Drag (Hot)
3. Angle Route (H Post)
4. RB Check Down

The Saints compress the formation by motioning in the receiver to the right get a bunch formation and a receiver in tight to the formation on the left. With the Giants primarily playing Man coverage on 3rd down, the tight formation gives the offensive players a more convenient way to get a free release. This 3rd down is no different, with the Giants Man coverage confirmed underneath with the motion while the 2 safeties guard the deep half's.

With the safeties playing over the top, Brees immediately comes of his 1st and 2nd read and looks to the shallow route then the trail route coming behind him. The inside receiver of the bunch fakes like he is running the out route, then plants his foot and cuts back inside with the defender a step behind him. Brees finds his man and the Saints have a 1st down.

3rd & 10   Ball on own 46   4th Quarter 7:58

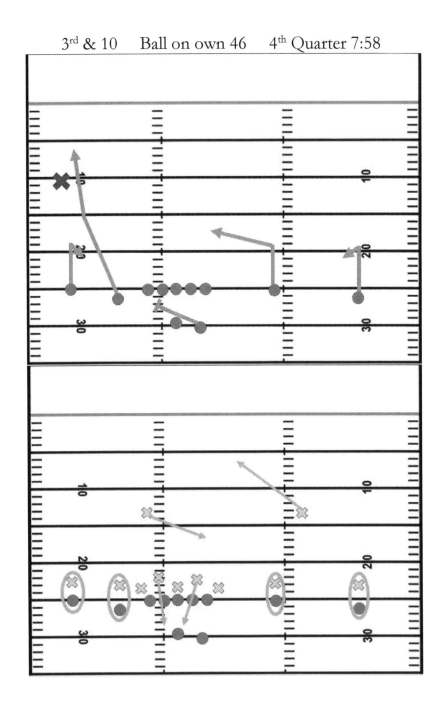

Facing a 3rd & long, the Saints come out with 2 receivers to each side of the formation with a FB to the right of Brees. The Giants show press coverage across the board with everyone on the line of scrimmage and 2 safeties deep.

The Saints call a quick game concept to both sides of the field. The quarterback determines pre-snap which side he wants to go with the ball.

At the snap, the Giants bring pressure up the middle and man up across the board. The boundary safety however buzzes down to the middle of the field as the field safety works over to the deep middle. Seeing this, Brees has a 1 on 1 with his fade route coming from the seam. He takes his shot but the defender does a great job of fighting through the ball and the pass falls incomplete.

3rd & 8   Ball on Giants 27   4th Quarter 3:05

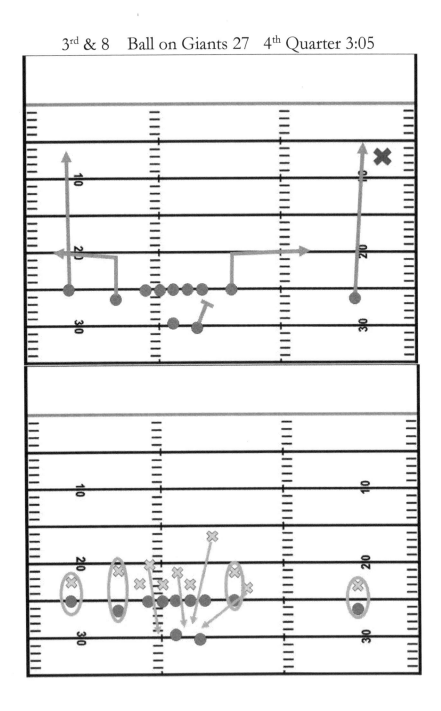

Facing yet another 3rd down the Saints come out with a TE and WR to the right with 2 WR to the left. Once again, the defense shows press man coverage and Brees knows the pressure is coming.

The Saints call a mirrored flat fade concept. This play works well against two high safety coverages, and man coverages.

Just as the Saints snap the ball, the FS starts sprinting down giving the Saints a true Cover 0 or man coverage with no over the top help. There is immediate pressure in Brees' face and he lets the ball go to the fade on the right. The receiver actually has a step on his defender but the rushed throw is underthrown allowing the defender to break the pass up.

Week 3 vs Atlanta

3rd & 2   Ball on own 33   1st Quarter 14:18

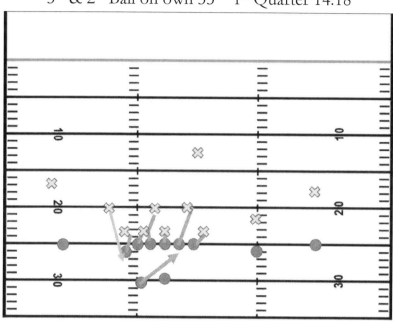

The Saints call inside zone on their first third down of the game. Calling inside zone with an H-back on the backside allows the offense to secure the backside for a cutback, which the running back takes advantage of on this play.

The Falcons are in a single high defense, playing a cover three zone with four down lineman. You will see this early and often from them.

Due to the single high structure, the Falcons will have an extra guy in the box to help out against the run. As the running back makes his cut, he is met by the strong safety (the unblocked defender).

The back is able to bounce off of this tackle just enough to pick up a first down.

3rd & 10   Ball on own 25   1st Quarter 5:13

Coverage Read:

Pick a matchup that you like, then make sure to look off the free safety to ensure one on one coverage.

The Saints call four verticals on third and long, a sound play call when expecting a single high safety (cover one or cover three).

The Falcons use a well-designed cover one robber/bracket scheme. The inside linebackers appear to be reading the centers drop. If the center turns towards you, you drop in coverage. If the center turns away from you, rush the quarterback.

The deep alignment of the linebackers hurts the chances of getting to the quarterback. The right tackle has plenty of time to react to the five technique dropping into coverage, and pick up the blitzer.

The Saints have two receivers running their routes in the same space, creating confusion when the ball is in the air. The pass falls incomplete bringing up a fourth down.

3rd & 7   Ball on own 39   2nd Quarter 13:28

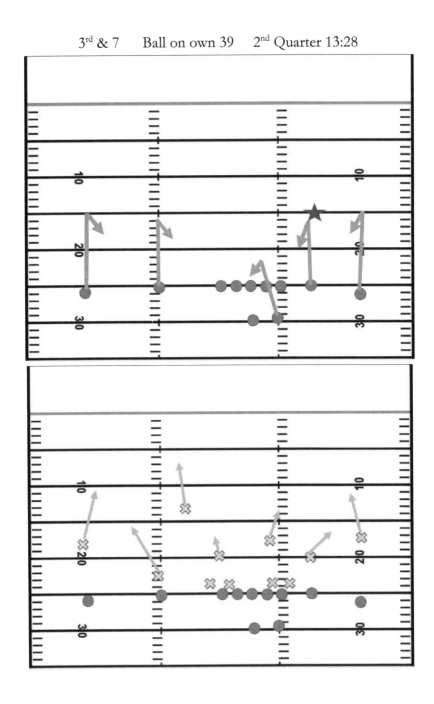

Combination Read

1. Pick a side pre-snap based on leverage and matchups
2. Inside Curl (7 yards)
3. Outside Curl (10 yards)

The Saints use a nice four vertical compliment, "All Stop" on this third down. The four vertical call on the previous third down was defended nicely, so the Saints figured the compliment would be open.

The Falcons call a soft cover three zone, with the flat defenders widening to get underneath any intermediate routes from the #1 receiver.

Brees times his feet up with the route progression nicely, and fits a good ball into the slot on the right. The receiver drops it, bringing up a fourth down.

3rd & 1   Ball on opponent 9   2nd Quarter 10:42

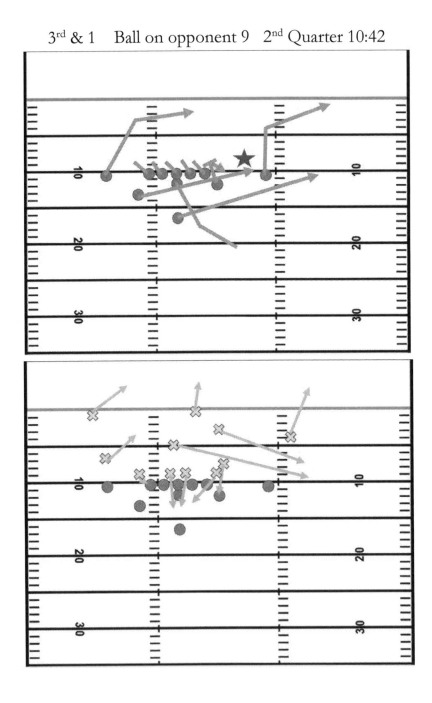

Progression Read:

1. Peak Corner
2. Tailback Flat
3. H-Back on left running the under flat
4. H-back on right chip blocking, releasing late

This short yardage play works well in the red zone. When the field shrinks vertically, the offense needs to explore a more horizontal attack. The three under routes stretch the underneath defenders and create confusion.

The Falcons play a cover three. two defenders react to the quick flat route from the tailback, leaving the under route open.

The Saints also used this play as their last 3rd down call against the Chargers in week 4. That time, the chip-release delay route opens up.

The Saints get the completion and pick up the first down.

3rd & 15   Ball on own 46   2nd Quarter 2:58

On third and long, the Saints call a drag screen. This is a conservative call that will either put the Saints in a position to go for it on fourth down, or punt.

The Falcons come out in a prevent-style cover four. They only rush 3, and drop an extra defender to fill an underneath hole in their zone. The linebackers and corners play it soft, understanding the down and distance needed.

The Saints pick up 8 yards, and are forced to punt of fourth down.

3rd & 8   Ball on own 27   3rd Quarter 11:39

Progression Read

1. Middle Crosser
2. Fade
3. Flat chip-release check down

The Saints call their middle read concept on this third down. The quarterback will read inside out, if the defense brackets his deep crosser, he will relocate to one of the outside fade routes.

The Falcons play a true man coverage. They press the point man in the bunch to avoid getting lost on any rub routes.

The QB sees that his deep crosser is bracketed with the robbing inside linebacker, so he resets his feet to find the fade on the left. The receiver gets a clean release off the ball and creates instant separation. The defender lunges forward at the receiver as he is making his cut. this creates the separation.

The Saints get a big play on a fantastic catch, and pick up the first down.

3rd & Goal   Ball on opponent 3   3rd Quarter 8:00

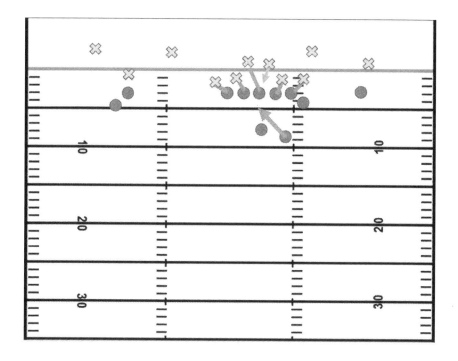

With the Falcons expecting pass on this third and goal, the Saints spread them out, and run inside zone.

The Saints leave the backside inside linebacker unblocked. The H-back attempt to cut him off, but has no chance even before the ball is snapped.

The inside linebacker dives at the running back's feet and misses the tackle. The Saints convert and score the touchdown.

3rd & 14   Ball on own 45   4th Quarter 15:00

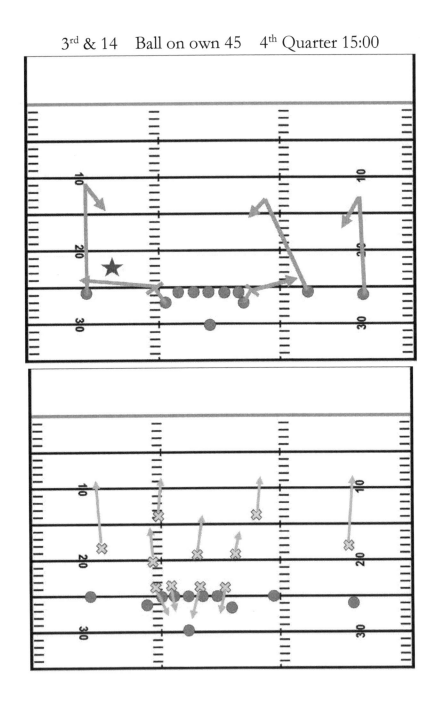

Progression Read (Inside-out):

1. Inside Curl
2. Outside Curl
3. Chip-release flat route

The Saints call their whole field Hank/ curl-flat concept on third and long, anticipating a soft zone from Atlanta.

The Falcons use a prevent style cover four defense, and rush four. The linebackers spot drop to a depth of about fifteen yards, right at the first down line. The thought process is to force the quarterback to take a check down, and rally up to make the tackle.

Brees cycles through his progressions, hesitates on the inside curl route, then settles for the check down in the flat on the left. The outside linebacker to the left is influenced by Brees pump faking the inside curl, and jumps to cover that route. The corner is blocked by the outside receiver, giving the Saints a nice lane to get to the first down marker.

After the receiver catches the ball, he moves quickly to pick up the first down.

3rd & 1   Ball on own 23   4th Quarter 6:24

Combination Read

1. Vs Single High Safety
   a. Read drop of OLB on right, throw flat or stick
2. Vs Two High Safeties: Read the drop of the middle linebacker
   a. Hit #3 if receiver can get inside separation on middle linebacker
   b. Hit #2 if #3 is covered

The Saints call Slants-Stick on third and short. The play has an answer for any zone, or man coverage. The most important part of the play for the offense is a quick release from the quarterback.

The Falcons call cover three, with a four man rush. The underneath defenders flat foot read the route stems of each receiver, understanding that the offense only needs one yard. This will allow them to break on any short routes.

The flat route gets leverage, as the outside linebacker / nickel hesitates for a quick second, and has to come from a depth of five yards. The quarterback gets the ball out of his hands quickly, and hits the running back for a first down.

3rd & 4   Ball on opponent 33   4th Quarter 4:42

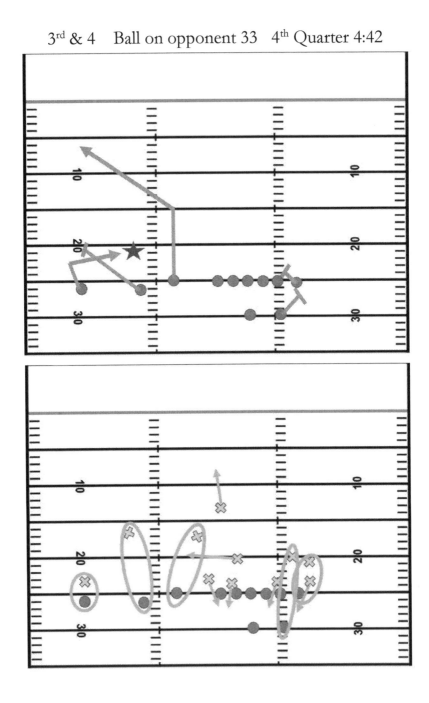

Progression Read

1. #1 on delayed slant
2. #2 on "pick" route
3. #3 on corner route

The Saints have a man to man beater called to the trips side of the formation. The two man combination on the outside is designed to pick the corner, and free up the #1 receiver on a delayed slant.

The Corner route by the third receiver is a nice way to incorporate a zone beater to the play. Zone defenders will see the pick routes, and trade off responsibilities. They will act more aggressively on these routes. They aren't as worried about another route entering their zone, since they see man beater routes.

The cornerback does a tremendous job of not getting picked by the #2 receiver. this puts him in a position to tackle the receiver, and force a fourth and one situation (The Saints pick up the first down on the following play with a QB sneak).

3ʳᵈ & 21   Ball on opponent 39   4ᵗʰ Quarter 3:16

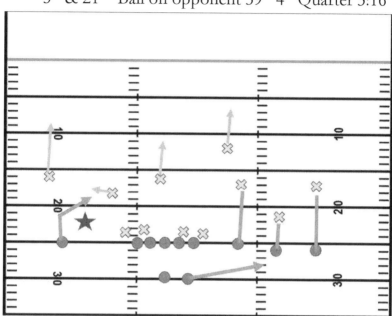

Progression Read

1. Slant
2. Swing Screen to Running Back

The Saints are in a third and long, with the game almost out of hand. They Saints use a quick pass play to try and pick up a few yards to make a fourth down attempt easier.

Brees throws the slant, with the flat defender waiting for the route. The receiver drops the ball with the defender looming, bringing up a fourth down.

.

Week 4 at San Diego

3rd & 6   Ball on own 39   1st Quarter 13:44

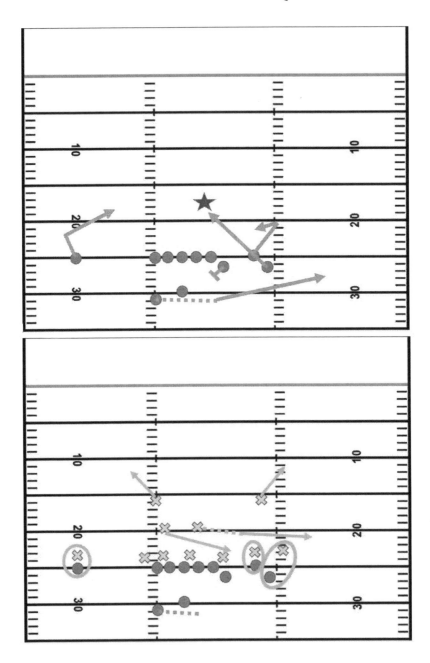

Progression Read:

1. Slant (#1 on QB's left)
2. Inside hook / slant (where QB threw the ball, #1 on QB's right)
3. Spot route
4. RB swing

The Saints call a variation off of their Hank concept. The motion of the runningback is meant to either remove a man defender from the box, or widen zone defenders to open up the hook routes.

The Chargers are in man coverage underneath, with two safeties to help over the top. Both inside linebackers react to the motion, which opens up the inside hook route. By the time the second guy realized he didn't need to follow the running back, it was too late.

The inside hook receiver notices it is man coverage and adjusts his route to stay on the move and run away from his defender. This results in a completion and a first down for the Saints.

3rd & 4   Ball on opponent 33   1st Quarter 12:01

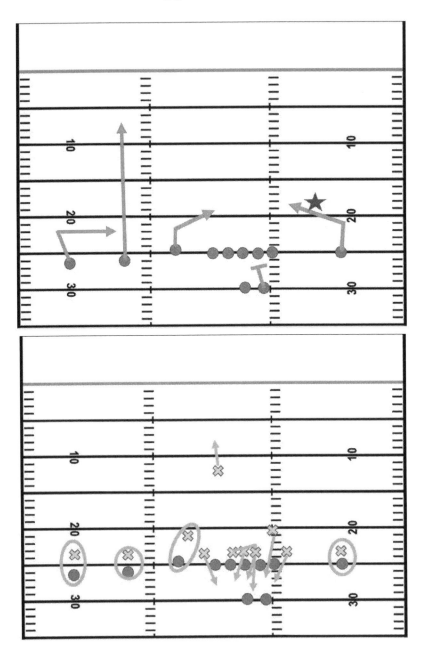

Progression Read

1. Slant (#1 on QB's right)
2. Slant (#3 on QB's left)
3. Seam
4. Drive

Brees makes an audible at the line, and changes the play once he sees San Diego lined up in press across the board, with a single safety.

The Chargers bring a five man rush, with three rushing to the quarterback's right. The Chargers would have gotten a free rusher on the quarterback had the 1 technique on the right guard stayed in his gap. Instead, he crosses over the center because he sees an opening on that side. This allows the right guard to peel off of him and pick up the twisting 1 technique from the other side of the center.

The single receiver away from the trips releases inside the pressed corner, and leans into him on his break. This creates the separation needed to fit the ball in. With a clear throwing lane and all six rushers picked up, Brees hits his receiver for a first down.

3rd & 4   Ball on own 26   1st Quarter 7:30

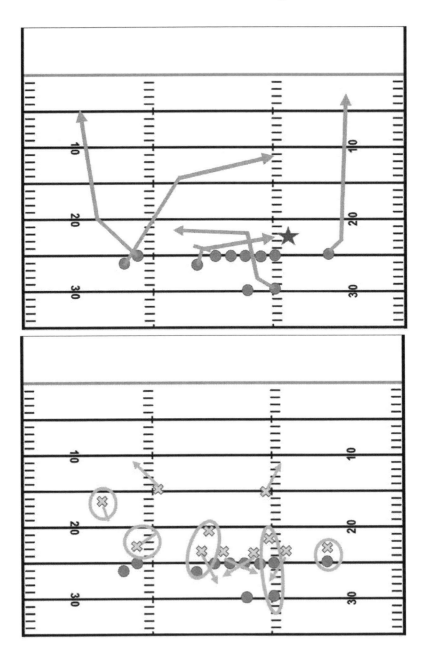

Progression Read

1. Wheel (on left side)
2. Deep Cross
3. TE drag
4. RB drag

The Chargers have called a variation of man coverage on the first two third downs of the game. The Saints call a common zone beater, Y Cross, with a twist to attack man coverage. The meshing of the underneath routes will give the play an added advantage against man.

After the ball is snapped, Brees sees man coverage and peeks at the wheel route on the left. Once he sees the deeper defender take the wheel, he looks to the deep crossing route. He knows the deep crosser will have a better angle to get to the middle of the field than the underneath defender.

Unfortunately for the Saints, the receiver goes out of his way to run into the defender, which throws off the timing on his deep crossing route. this could have easily been avoided.

The tight end is able to create separation due to the play design. Typically when an H back chips an defensive end, he will then run a hitch or flat route. As the tight end is chipping the end, the linebacker shuffles outside to be prepared for the flat route. This gives the tight end the inside leverage he needs.

Brees side steps some pressure, and dumps the ball off to his tight end for a first down.

3rd & 10   Ball on own 33   1st Quarter 6:00

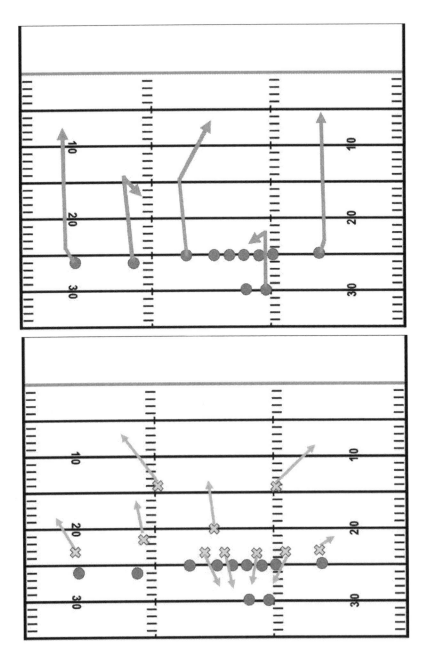

Coverage Read:

- Read away from safety rotation vs single high safety.
- Reade spacing of safeties against two high safeties.
- RB check down

After getting burned playing man on the first three third downs of the game, the Chargers play cover two. The Saints call a four vertical concept on this third and long. The routes convert to what you see in the diagram against cover two.

The Chargers do a great job of taking away any window Brees would need to fit a ball into one of the holes in the cover two zone. With the safeties widening and the middle linebacker gaining depth, Brees does not have access to any of his vertical options. As he resets his feet to look at the curl route, he gets sacked.

3rd & 1   Ball on own   1st Quarter 0:26

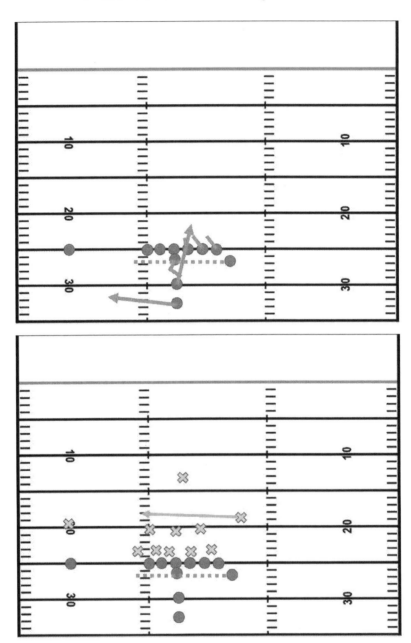

The Saints call a fullback dive on third and one. The play is called to the side with a gap open, which allows the right guard and right tackle to double team the D-lineman lined up over the right guard.

Right before the ball is snapped a linebacker comes down and lines up in the C gap to the offense's right. The tight end blocks down on him to give the fullback a wall to get the needed yardage.

The Saints get just enough surge to pick up a first down.

3rd & 13   Ball on own 33   2nd Quarter 14:02

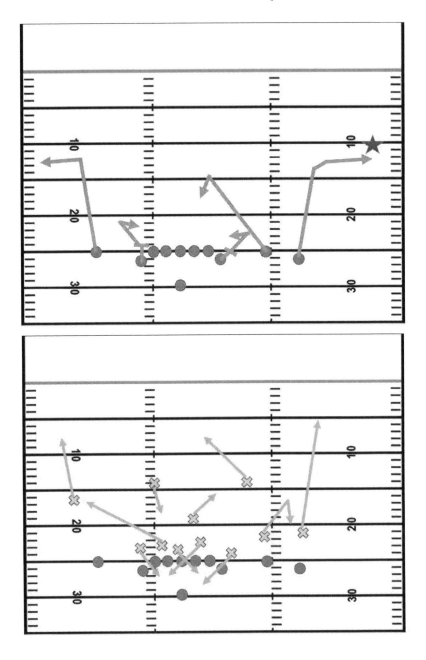

Progression Read:

1. Deep out route
2. Inside curl
3. Check down hook on chip release

    The Saints call a 5 man horizontal stretch on third and long. This stretch, much like their whole field curl flat (Hank) concept, is meant to defeat a cover three, which has four underneath defenders.

    With the chargers calling cover three, this play is a well-timed call. In a third and long situation, the defense should be defending any vertical stems with more intensity than they would on a first or second down. They are typically taught to react to any underneath route after the ball has been thrown.

    The flat defender on the right gets caught making a mistake. Instead of continuing on his path to undercut the deep out route by the outside receiver, he sees the back chip-releasing to the flat.

    This hesitation allows the QB to throw the out route on time, and pick up a first down.

3rd & 7   Ball on opponent 46   2nd Quarter 12:29

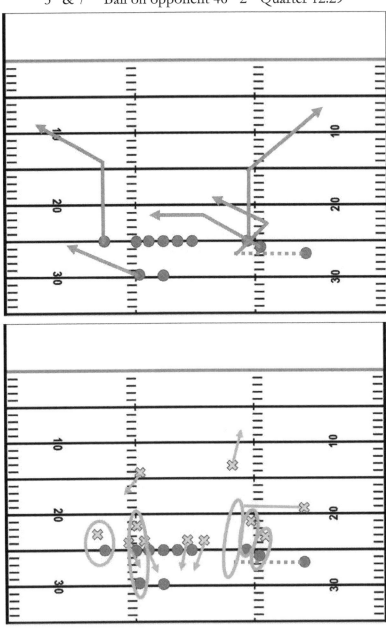

Progression Read:

1. Post route (motion man)
2. Drag
3. RB Swing

The Saints call the "H Post" concept on this third down. The motion man, running the "post" route, has options on which way he can break his route. the routes that surround the "post" are meant to replace defenders if they bracket the "post" route.

Once again, the matchup of play calls favors the Saints. With the Chargers calling a true man coverage, the motion to bunch and switch releases puts a lot of pressure on the defense to react to the breaks of each route.

The point man in the bunch set does a nice job of walling off the defender guarding the post route. This allows the QB to hit the post route for another first down.

3rd & 3   Ball on opponent 4   2nd Quarter 9:45

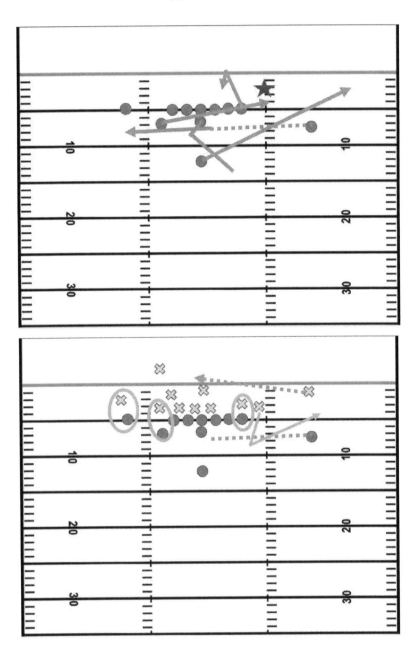

Progression Read:

1. RB flat route
2. H-back on the "under" route
3. Tight end on hitch route

The Saints use a creative play call to get a touchdown on a third down in the red zone (essentially third and goal). The jet sweep play action, combined with two receivers in the flat with a rub route from the play side tight end gives the Saints an easy touchdown.

The offensive line reach blocks to their left to give the play action some sizzle. The tight end on the play side runs a hitch route over the next inside defender (middle linebacker) to create a natural "rub" for the crossing H-back. The receiver on the left takes the play off and does not run a route.

The running back releasing quickly into the flat will pull away any zone flat defender, and the man guarding him if it is man to man.

The Chargers defense does not have much of a chance, and the Saints convert for the easy touchdown.

3rd & 9   Ball on own 12   2nd Quarter 3:43

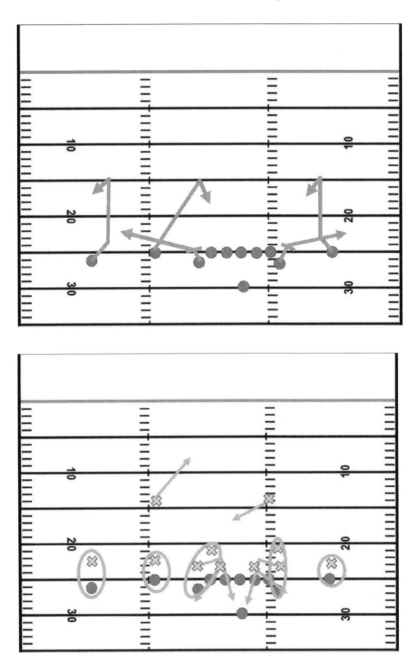

Progression Read

1. Inside curl
   (Read the side that the inside curl is pressured from)
2. Curl
3. Flat

The Saints run the whole field curl flat, or Hank concept. The play works best against soft zones, particularly cover 3.

The Chargers run a cover 1 with the strong safety robbing the #2 receiver on the offense's left. This is a smart tactic, as the Saints will often run crossing routes with this receiver.

The best way to get pressure on a stationary quarterback is right up the middle, and that is what the Chargers did on this play. The two stunts give the Saint's guards fits, and Brees is sacked, forcing a punt.

3rd & 8   Ball on opponent 47   3rd Quarter 12:57

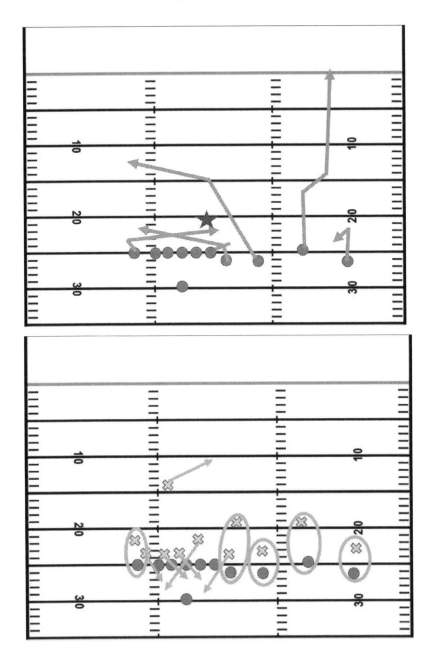

Progression Read:

1. Slot fade
2. Hitch
3. Drag (left to right)

The Saints call the mesh concept out of a quads formation. They use a two man flat fade variation as the first read in the progression, with a drag route entering the QB's vision as the 3rd read, or check down. This concept creates a nice triangle read for the quarterback.

The Chargers rush five, and play a pure cover 1 behind it.

The play call for the Saints works out nicely against man coverage. The slot fade is a good primary target for big-play opportunity. The vertical route has the added bonus of the extra space afforded by the slot position. The Chargers are also aware of this, and place the DB in a great position to defend this route. The DB plays with inside leverage and is quick to open his hips to run with the route. This film is great teaching tape for DB's trying to defend the slot fade route.

The tight end on the left side of the formation wins his matchup on a delayed drag route, which gives the Saints another first down.

3rd & 3   Ball on opponent 5   3rd Quarter 9:44

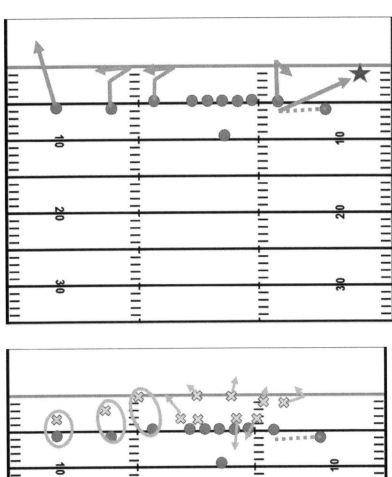

Progression Read

1. Flat
2. Stick
3. Whips

Out of an empty formation, the Saints run whips to the trips side, and a two man stick concept to the two receiver side.

The Chargers only rush three, and keep a few extra defenders to help on inside breaking routes.

When the Chargers see the motion, they make an in-out call on the two receiver stack. This gives the stick route the outside leverage it needs for the route to open up. The tight end runs a great route and creates separation from his man.

Brees feels the corner cheating back to rob the stick route. Without resetting his feet, he gets the ball to the flat.

After an accurate throw from the QB, the receiver breaks the initial contact to lean forward for a first down.

3rd & 6   Ball on 34   3rd Quarter 7:34

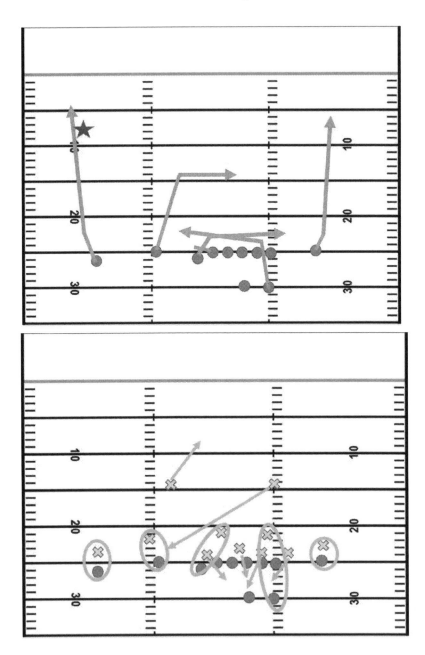

Progression Read:

1. Deep Cross
   Read the side that the route is getting squeezed from next
2. Go route
3. Drag check down

The Saints call the "middle read" concept here. The play is designed to get the ball to the slot in the middle of the field. If he is covered, either the outside receiver will have a one on one, or the checkdown route will be uncovered.

The Chargers have the perfect defense called for this; Cover 1 with a cross bracket on the slot running the deep crossing route. the opposite safety does a nice job of cutting this route off, forcing the QB to look elsewhere.

Brees resets his eyes to the go route down the left sideline. The receiver is not expecting the ball to come his way, and the ball falls incomplete and brings up a fourth down.

3ʳᵈ & 8   Ball on own 28

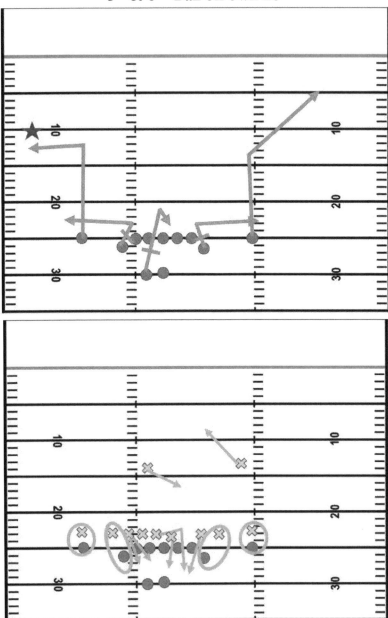

Coverage Read

1. Read away from the rotation of safeties
2. Progression read: Corner/comeback
3. Check down (chip-release flat routes)

The Saints are trying to isolate the outside receivers on the corners with this play. The tight split gives the receiver a two way go, which makes the corner's job more difficult.

Getting a good jam on the outside receivers is a must for the corner backs. They in fact get a good jam, and it messes up the timing with the quarterback. Brees steps up to buy himself time, but at that point, he is facing pressure in his face. He underthrows his receiver to the left, bringing up a fourth down.

3rd & 6   Ball on own 44   4th Quarter 7:04

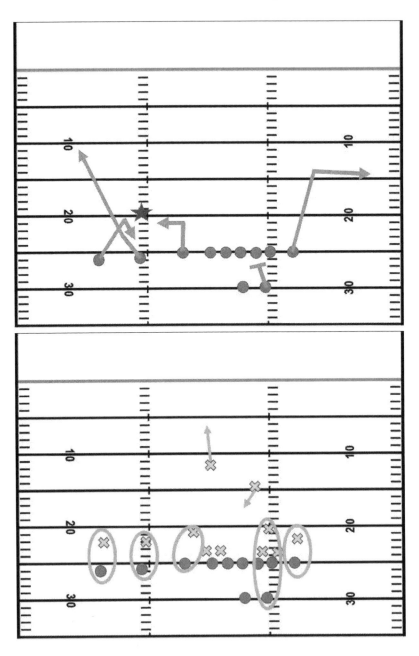

The Saints make an autible at the line once they see man coverage. They check to a two man"pick" concept on the left.

The play appears to be a broken play, as the #3 receiver on the left runs a stick route, which runs into the angled hitch route from the #1 receiver.

The Chargers make a switch call on the #1 and #2 receivers to the left, which takes away the wheel route. The QB is forced to check it down to one of the underneath routes.

As the ball is thrown, two receivers are in the area, and the ball falls incomplete forcing a fourth down.

3rd & 4   Ball on opponent 7   4th Quarter 5:44

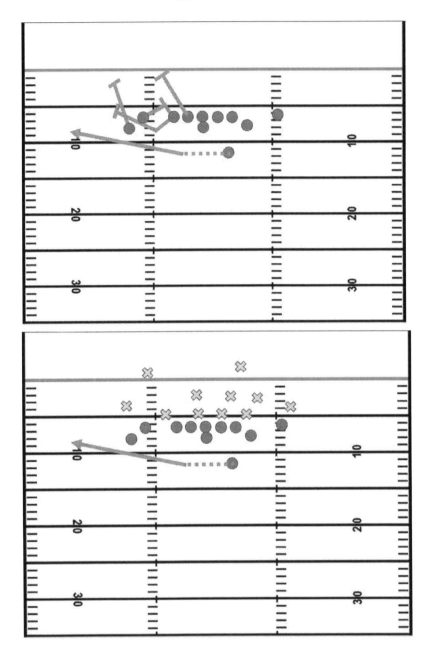

The Saints call a quick-motion toss play on this third down in the red zone. The offset back usually indicates something quick to that side of the field. So instead, the Saints motion him away and attack quickly to the other side.

The blocking scheme is the same as their normal toss scheme, a crack block from a receiver or tight end, and the play side tackle pulling. This play is a great way to get the ball on the edge quickly. It also forces defensive backs to come up and tackle a running back in space.

The cornerback does a nice job of stringing the play out as long as he can. The safety and 1 technique do a great job of flowing to the ball. The Chargers make the tackle, and stop the Saints short of a first down.

3rd & 2   Ball on opponent 23   4th Quarter 3:59

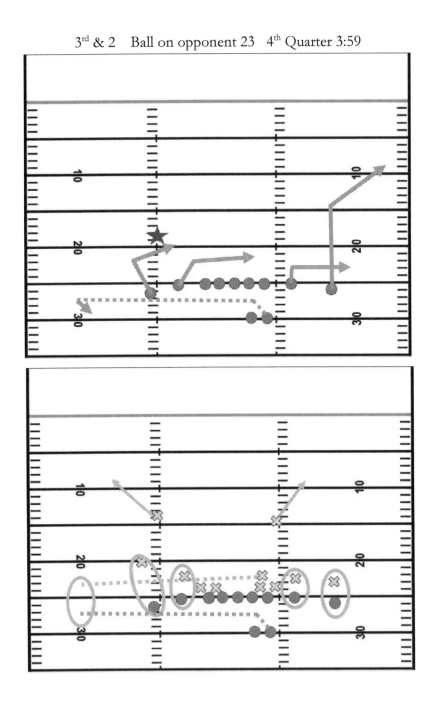

Progression Read:

1. Post Route (slant route)
2. Drag Route
3. Flat Route

At a critical moment in the game, the Saints turn to the "H post concept". They used this play earlier in the game, on page 96 with success.

Once Brees sends the runningback in motion, he sees a linebacker go with him. This is a tell-tale sign of man coverage. at this moment, Brees knows he is probably going to hit the post route.

The man guarding the post route runner seems to be expecting the "slot fade" route. He is playing off coverage, even with two safeties behind him to help on deep routes. He reacts to the post route flat-footed.

Brees hits the post route to pick up another first down, and bring the Saints closer to converting a game winning drive.

3rd & 1   Ball on opponent 4   4th Quarter 2:21

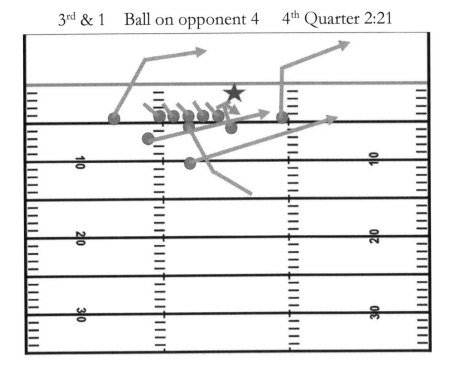

Progression Read

1. Corner Route
2. Tailback in flat
3. H-back on under route
4. H-back on chip release hitch

As the Chargers scramble to set their defense, Brees gets up to the line quickly and calls this creative play action concept on third and one in the red zone.

The Chargers do not get their defense set, and have to react to the flow of the play. fortunately for them, all of their linebackers flow with the backfield action, and cut off the first two flat routes.

The H-back on the right chip releases, and breaks open. Brees appears to throw him the ball, but the other H-back turns around and catches the ball behind him. The Saints pick up the first down, and get stopped just short of the end one.

Week 6 vs Carolina

3rd & 1   Ball on own 43   1st Quarter 13:33

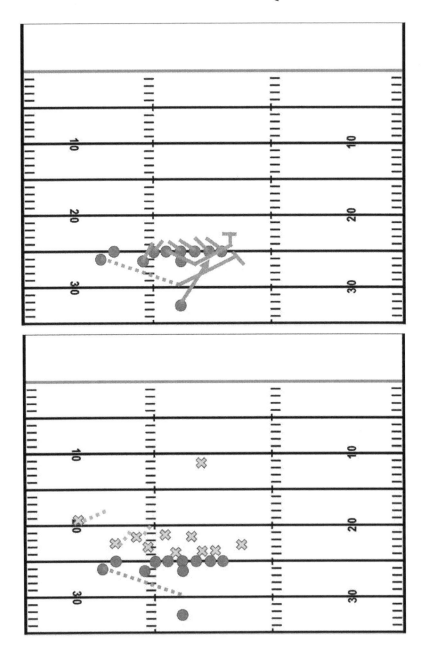

The Saints run power on their first third down of the game. They start with the strength of the formation to the offense's left, then motion the fullback into the backfield to get the extra blocker to run power to the weak side. .

The fullback gets a nice block, along with the right tackle and right guard. The tight end struggles with the 5 technique, and he gets some penetration to disrupt the play.

The left guard gets distracted by this penetration, but continues on his path to make a key block on the filling linebacker.

The Saints get enough push up front, and pick up the first down.

3rd & 6   Ball on opponent 22   1st Quarter 11:04

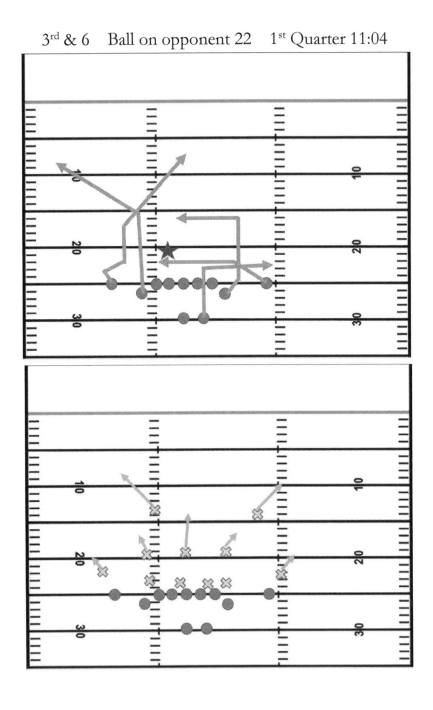

Progression Read

1. Corner
2. Post
3. Drag
4. Dig
5. RB checkdown

The Saints call a scissors concept to the frontside (left side) and a drive concept on the backside. The drive concept compliments scissors well because the drag and dig will enter the QB's vision as he is coming off of the corner and post. The post route will delay his release slightly and run his route underneath the corner route.

The Panthers show blitz, then back off and play cover two.

The corner back bails and sits under the corner route, which allows the safety to play the post route. Brees hits his drag route, but he gets tackled before he can get past the chains.

3rd & 2   Ball on opponent 3   1st Quarter 9:55

The Saints run a quick hitting run on third and short near the goal line. With the intention of going for it on 4th down if they don't convert, the Saints run a safe play that would not put them in a worse situation for 4th down.

The offensive line blocks inside zone to their left, trying to create a wall for the back to squeak out a few extra yards.

The Panthers crash quickly. With the left inside linebacker being unblocked, he is able to stand firm and force a fourth down.

4th & 1   Ball on opponent 2   1st Quarter 9:20

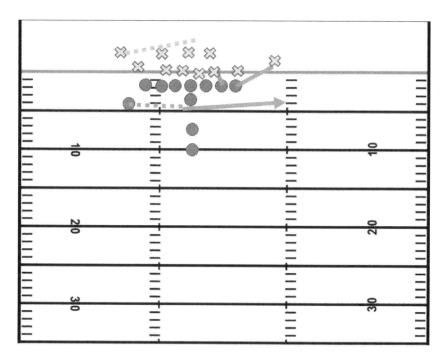

The Saints call a jet sweep on 4th down deep in the red zone. The Panthers are packing the box to stuff the inside run, and are playing man coverage on the outside. This makes the jet sweep an optimal play call.

The Saints leave the 6 technique unblocked. The man guarding the jet sweeper can not keep pace with the motion, and the Saints score an easy touchdown on a very creative play call.

3rd & 9   Ball on own 5   1st Quarter 4:36

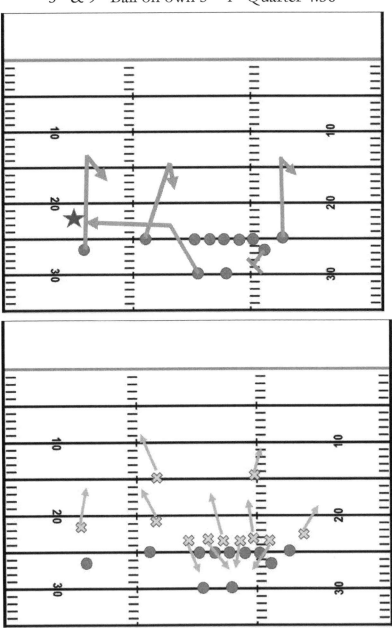

Progression Read: Inside –Out

1. Inside Curl
2. Outside Curl on the left
3. Flat route

The Saints run one of their staple concepts on third and long. This Hank/Curl flat concept is one of their go-to concepts, especially on third downs.

The Panthers have the perfect defense called, cover two. The pressure look that they show before the snap forces the Saints to keep an extra blocker in for protection.

This film can be great teaching tape for how to defend the curl flat concept with cover two. The Panthers spot drop to get depth, and force the QB to throw the ball underneath the first down marker.

The Saints get a completion to the check down, but do not get the first down.

3rd & 5   Ball on own 12 1st Quarter 3:04

Many offensive coordinators save their shot plays for first and second down, and play the sticks on third down. Using a double move on a third down can bring added benefits that can not be found on earlier downs.

With the defense defending the first down line with more intent on these third downs, a double move has a better chance of getting a defender to bite.

The Panthers use a quarters coverage, with a center read blitz. The linebackers lined up in the A-gap read the center. If the center turns toward you, you drop into coverage. If the center turns away from you, you rush the QB. This forces the fullback to stay in protection, while only rushing three.

Despite having deep responsibilities, the corner jumps the out route at the sticks. The Saints hit the homerun and score a touchdown.

3rd & 1   Ball on opponent 20   2nd Quarter 14:40

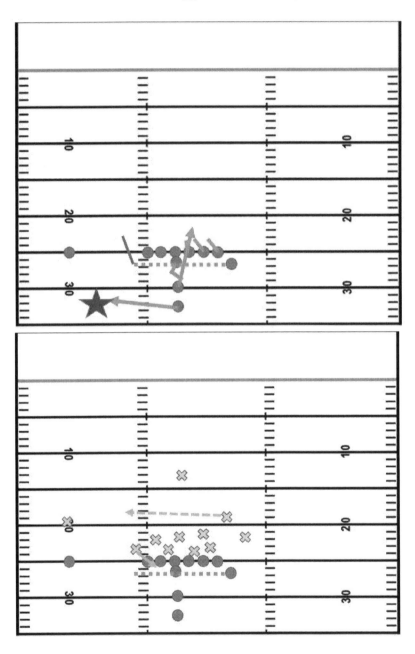

One of the Saints' go-to short yardage packages is the fullback dive/ tailback flip series. On this play, the Siants go to the tailback flip.

The Panthers are playing man to man, as the Saints identify with motion. The linebackers hesitate with the dive fake, which prevents them from getting to the edge. The defensive end crashes down, creating a nice lane for the toss action.

The Saints get a good block from their motion man, and spring the tailback to a big gain and a first down.

3rd & 5   Ball on own 25   2nd Quarter 7:54

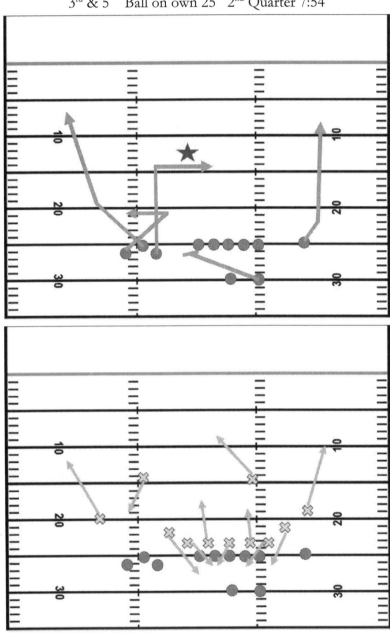

Progression Read

1. Fade (receiver on right)
2. Dig
3. Wheel
4. Whip

The Saints run a bunch concept meant to place the middle linebacker in a high – low conflict. The whip and dig will put him in a position to have to commit to one or the other. This play is a good call for 3rd and five, as the underneath whip route (checkdown) has a chance of converting if left open.

The Panthers call a creative fire zone blitz (5 rushers, 3 short zones, 3 deep zones). The nose guard rushes opposite the center's shuffle, forcing the back to stay in to protect.

The whip route gets the attention of the middle hook defender, opening up a nice window for the dig route. Brees evades some pressure and hits the dig route for a first down.

3rd & 1   Ball on opponent 35   2nd Quarter 5:05

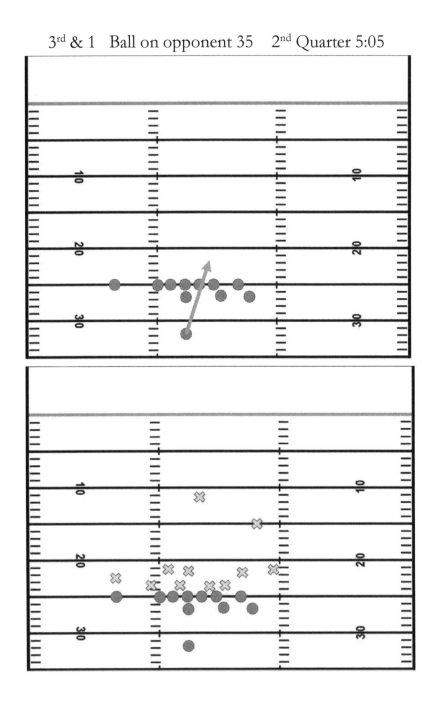

The Saints play some smashmouth football on this third and one. This dive play was used on a third down in their first drive as well.

The Panthers stay in their base defense. They were probably thinking that the Saints would try something creative, and wanted to make sure they didn't have any glaring mismatches in the passing game.

The nose guard (1 technique) does a tremendous job of not giving ground on the double team. As the left guard peels off to get the linebacker, the nose guard disengages from the center to make the tackle at the line of scrimmage.

The Panthers hold strong on third down, and force a field goal attempt.

3rd & 15   Ball on own 13   2nd Quarter 2:48

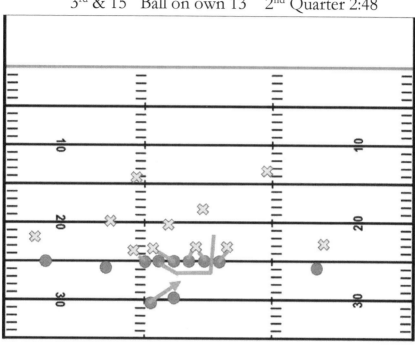

The Saints call 1-back power on this third and long. The Panthers call a conservative cover two, with the linebackers playing off the ball.

The fronstide double team (right guard & right tackle) stay endgaged, and do not feel off to get the middle linebacker. This forces the running back to bounce it outside.

The safety and corner fill the alley nicely, and force a furth down.

3ʳᵈ & 7   Ball on own 15   12:02

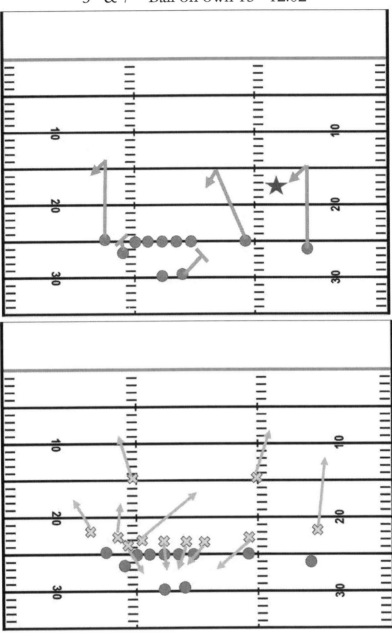

Progression Read:

1. Inside Curl
2. Outside Curl
3. TE Turn Route

The Saints call their whole field curl-flat concept again out of the same formation, only flipped for the hash mark. This time, they have to keep their back in for protection as the Panthers bring a field blitz. The Saints do a nice job picking up the blitz.

The Panthers seem to have a busted coverage. They have no underneath help on their left side, leaving the outside curl route wide open.

Brees recognizes the coverage lapse, and hits the oitside reciever to pick up the first down.

3rd & 14   Ball on 50   2nd Quarter 5:04

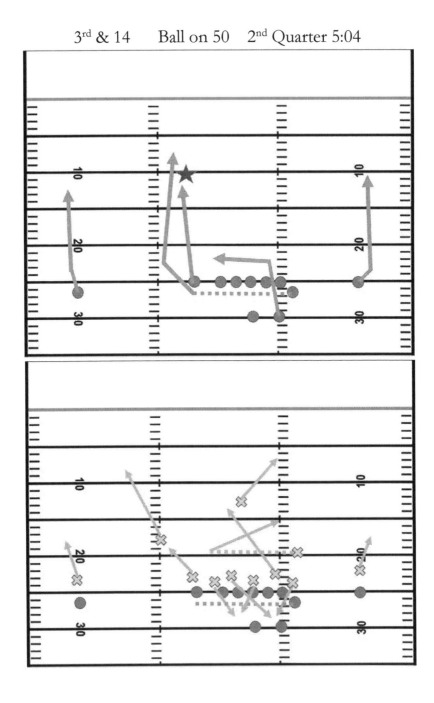

The Saints call four verticals on this third and long. The motion gets the slot a free release to run his vertical stem, and gets him down the field quicker.

The panthers do a nice job of disguising their cover two. They send the nickel across the field with the motion, making the QB think that they are playing man. At the snap of the ball, the nickel roams back to defend the weak hook zone.

The Saints end up with a broken play. The two slots end up in essentially the same spot in the middle of the field, both running the split adjustment against two high safeties. Only one them should be in this spot.

Sometimes its better to be lucky than good. The throw from Brees to fit the ball in the tight window is incredible. He makes a back shoulder throw on the deep-dropping Tampa two technique from the middle linebacker. The ball floats into the tight end's arms and the Saints end up scoring a touchdown.

3rd & 20   Ball on own 5   3rd Quarter 1:48

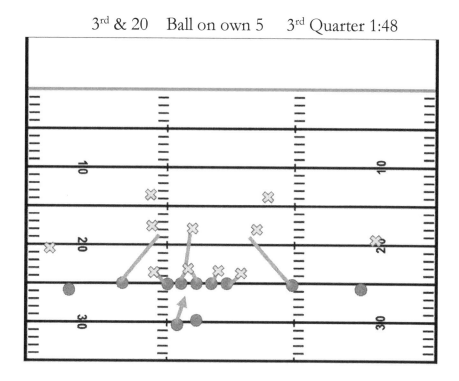

The Saints call a draw play on third and forever to try to give their punter some more room.

The 1 technique and 5 technique on the defense's right do a nice job of shedding their blocks to make the play, forcing a fourth down.

3ʳᵈ & 3   Ball on own 32   4ᵗʰ Quarter 8:29

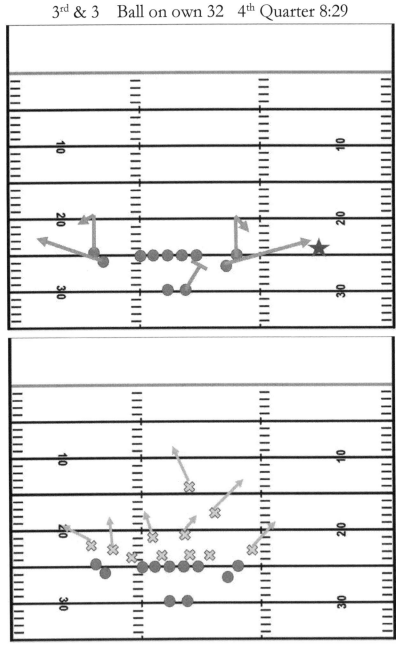

Combination Read:

1. Pick a side based on presnap alignment
2. Flat route
3. Stick route

The Saints call a quick-hitting, mirrored, two man stick concept out of a compressed 2x2 formation. The routes are meant to attack soft zone-dropping linebackers and corners.

The Panthers call a disguised cover two. The underneath zone defenders drop to about five yards, which gives the offense an easy way to pick up the first down.

Brees hits the flat route on the right for a quick completion, and pick up just enough yards for the first down.

3rd & 3   Ball on opponent 7   4th Quarter 6:10

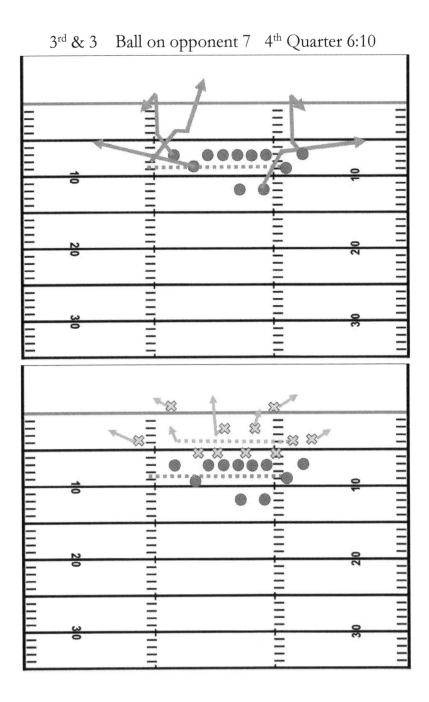

Progression Read

1. Hank & Go (double move)
2. Turn Curl
3. Flat

The Saints pull out another double move, this time in the red zone. Using your best "shot" plays in high leverage situations gives your offense a great chance of striking gold. They called the base play (Hank/Curl Flat) several times on third downs earlier in the game.

The Panthers disguise their cover two, once again. This time they send a guy to shadow the motion man, simulating man coverage. The safeties and corners don't play a true cover two. They are adapting their coverage to their location on the field. They zone drop to the goal line, and react to the routes around them.

The Panthers cover up all three of the reads on the left, and force the QB to extend the play. The middle linebacker does an outsanding job of positioning himself to defend the Hank route, and the double move

The play then breaks down, and Brees hits the flat route runner in the back of the end zone for a touchdown.

3rd & 10   Ball on own 25   4th Quarter 2:00

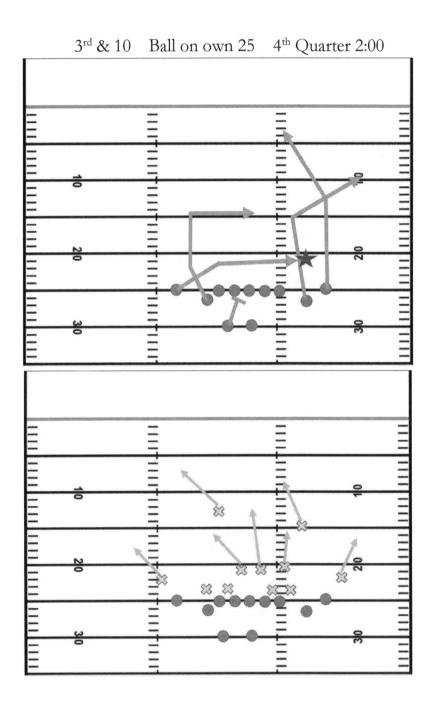

Progression Read

1. Glance Post
2. Corner Route
3. Drag
4. Dig

The Saints run the scissors concept with a backsdie drag and dig on this important third down, with the game tied. The play is a simple progression for the QB, that is sound against most coverages.

The Panthers call a cover two, once again. This one is hard to tell if it is infact a cover two, based on the way the left corner and outside linebacker drop. The deep drop of the middle linebacker into the middle hole gives away the tampa two coverage.

Against a cover two, the backside combination will typically be what is open. The underneath coverage clears out for the drag, that picks up the first down.

3rd & 7   Ball on opponent 40   4th Quarter 0:26

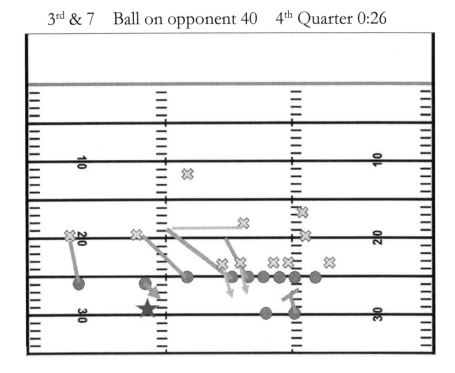

With only 26 seconds left in the game, the Saints call a slot screen. This call is a conservative one. Meant to pick up yards and make the game winning field goal easier.

The play picks up six yards, and gives the Saints the yardage they need to hit the game winning field goal.

Week 7 at Kansas City

3rd & 3   Ball on opponent 45   1st Quarter 8:24

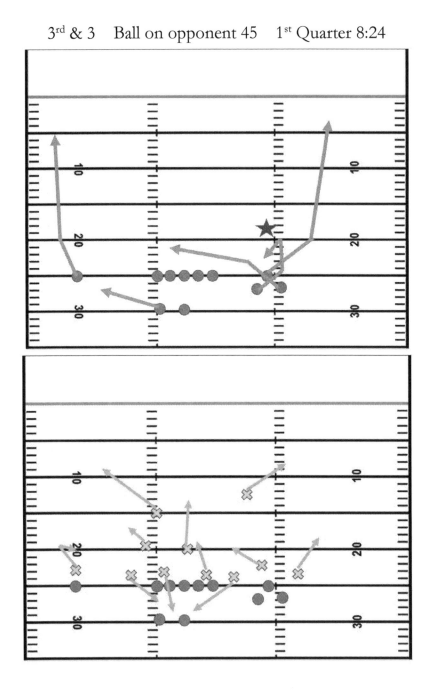

Progression Read

1. Drag
2. Spot
3. RB Swing

The Saints run a variation of the old "H Post" concept. This concept was made famous by Mike Martz's offense in the late 1990's and early 2000's. The receiver running the spot route is most likely running an option route. In this case, he sits in the void created by the drag and wheel routes.

The Saints call a drop 8 Tampa two coverage. This coverage is identical to the traditional Tampa two, with a defensive lineman filling in the middle hook zone for the vacating middle linebacker.

Theoretically, this coverage should cover this concept nicely. The dropping defensive lineman will wall off the drag route, and allow the strong hook defender to play the spot route. This defender gets distracted with the drag route, and then focuses his eyes on the QB.

Brees hits the spot route to pick up the first down.

3rd &4   Ball on own 30   1st Quarter 3:03

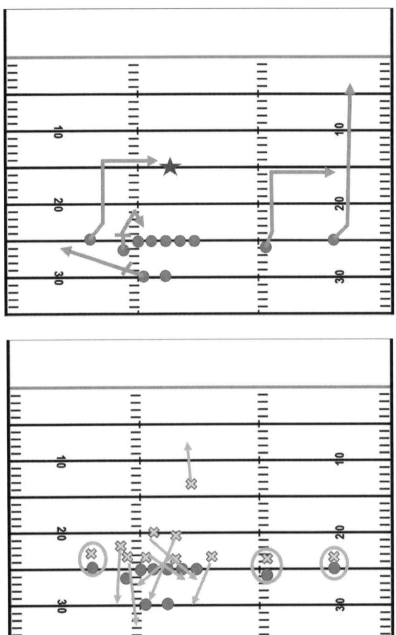

Progression Read

1. 10 Yard out
2. Dig
3. TE on chip release hitch route
4. RB on chip release swing route

The chiefs come out in a cover 1 press man look. They bring both inside linebackers on a cross blitz after the ball is snapped. This. play shows how the Saints like to handle blitz situations. Instead of the traditional response of keeping extra blockers in to max protect, they like to instead "chip".

It is important to understand the difference between "check release" and "chip release" for attached tight ends and running backs (terminology can vary, but it is important to understand the definitions). Check releases will have the back read a linebacker, and if that linebacker blitzes, they will stay and block them. A "chip release" will have the back block the 5 or 7 tech for a split second, and then release into their route. This gives the quarterback the time he needs to look at his primary options, and then dump the ball down to the "chippers" if they are uncovered due to a blitz.

With a few extra defenders rushing, the check release from the tight end gives Brees the extra second he needs to get to his second read on the play, the dig route. Without the chip, Brees would have had an unblocked defender in his face. The tight end that check-releases ends up uncovered once he gets into his route.

The key to this play is the Chiefs having no rusher in the A gap between the center and right guard. Instead, they have two in the adjacent B gap. This gives Brees the time he needs, and a window to step up and see the dig route.

This play is a great call against a single high safety. Unfortunately for the Saints, this play gets called back due to a penalty. This puts the Saints in another third down situation.

3rd & 9   Ball on own 25   1st Q 2:56

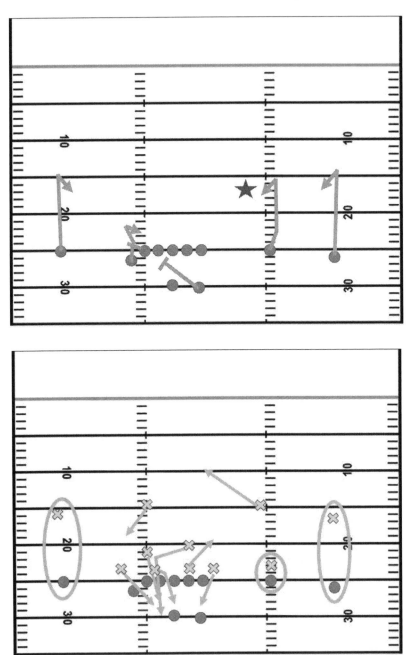

Combination Read:

- Read the side of the field with the largest cushion.
- If the defense doesn't blitz, the back has the ability to check down and replace vacating linebackers

The penalty pushed the Saints back five yards. The Chiefs come with another single high safety blitz with man coverage behind it. The man to man defenders are flat-foot reading at the same depth of the first down marker (8-10 yards).

The Chiefs bring four rushers to the offense's left side, and get a free rusher to the quarterback. The thought process is that the blitz will force the quarterback to throw the ball sooner than he wants, and the loose man technique will allow the defense to make a tackle short of the first down line.

The Saints run another good concept against single high coverage. The stop routes are good against singled-up corners that are looking to prevent any big plays down the field.

With the Chiefs looking to prevent a first down, they are sitting on the outside stop routes. Brees then looks to his slot receiver, and releases the ball just before he gets hit to convert the play into a first down. If Kansas City showed their blitz a split second sooner, the play most likely would have resulted in a 4th down instead.

3rd & 12   Ball on own 39   1st Quarter 0:58

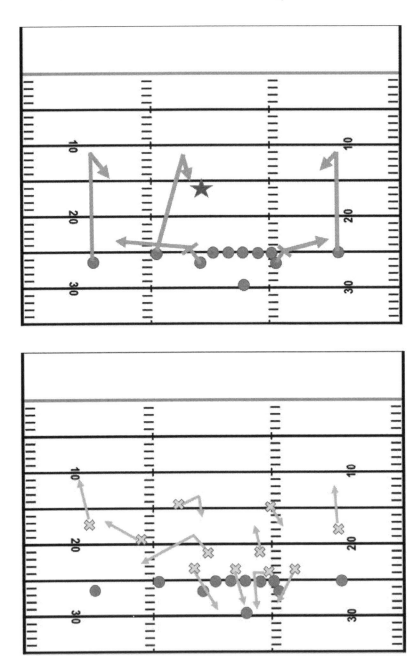

Progression read

1. Inside Curl
    (QB then picks a side)
2. Outside curl
3. Flat route

The Saints run a whole field curl-flat concept. This play is a longer version of the spacing concept they will typically use in first and second down situations. The play includes two chip blocks from the flat route runners to give the QB an extra second to sit on the deeper curl routes.

The Chiefs run what appears to be a cover three, which is the optimal coverage for this concept. There is communication between the safeties and linebackers right as the ball is snapped, so there could be some confusion as to what exactly the coverage is supposed to be. Nobody breaks to the flat on the offense's right.

The two inside hook defenders split and create a void for the inside curl route. Exactly how the play is drawn up, Brees throws the curl route right out of the break.

The free safety is playing aggressively, and is flat foot reading the route at the first down marker. The ball is tipped by the receiver, and intercepted and returned for a touchdown.

3ʳᵈ & 2   Ball on own 33   2ⁿᵈ Quarter 15:00

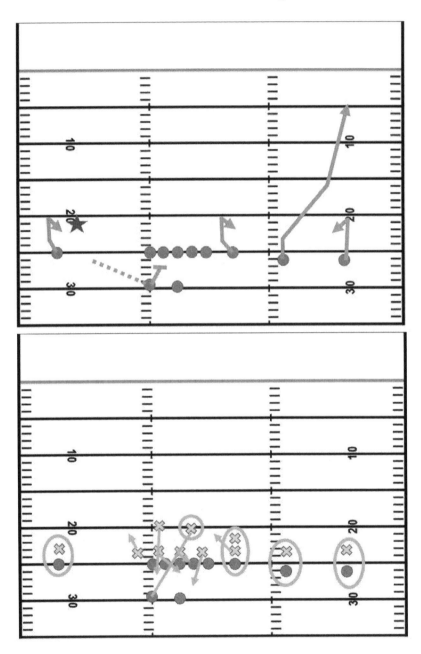

The Saints shift their running back into the backfield to try and get a clue as to what the Chiefs are doing. Brees sees the Chiefs in a press man cover zero look. And makes an audible.

The Chiefs only end up rushing four out of their bear front - cover zero look. The two ends drop back to rob an inside breaking routes.

The Saints run the spade concept to their right, and a hitch route to the left. Brees determines pre-snap that the hitch route is where he wants to go.

The singled up corner has no choice but to turn his hips with the vertical release, as he has no help over the top. Brees hits the receiver out his break to pick up the first down.

3rd & 17   Ball on own 30   2nd Quarter 13:00

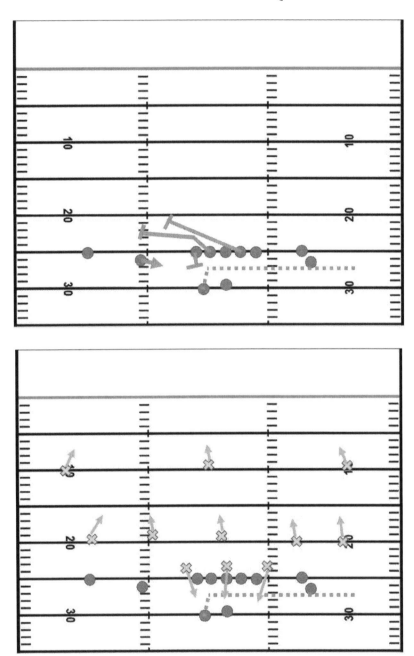

For this third and long situatuiuon, the Saints play it conservative and call a quick jailbreak screen to their slot receiver.

The Chiefs call a drop-8 Tampa Two coverage in order to tighten the throwing windows for Brees. The three deep defenders start the play at the first down marker, and give a slight backpedal after the ball is snapped. The underneath defenders do the same.

After the ball is thrown, the middle linebacker overpursues and gives the receiver space to cut back to the middle of the field after the catch. The center is unable to cut off the right outside linebacker, who makes the tackle nine yards downfield.

3rd 13   Ball on own 32   2nd Quarter 5:33

The Saints call four verticals out of a half-compressed bunch to the right, with the runningback motioning out of the backfield to run the outside vertical to the left.

You can tell that the Saints did not use route conversions on this play because of the routes that the outside receivers ran. Both continued on their vertical path, even with the corner bailing with his hips open the entire time.

The Chiefs run a pattern match cover three. The flat defenders for the Chiefs play the slot receivers with outside leverage, and both run with the seam routes. The third receiver to the right chipped the defensive end before running a drag route. The middle hook defenders do not gain much depth, probably because the flat defenders will carry any seam routes. The hook defender on the right breaks on the drag route and makes the tackle for a nine yard completion, short of a first down.

3rd & 10   Ball on own 48   2nd Quarter 1:00

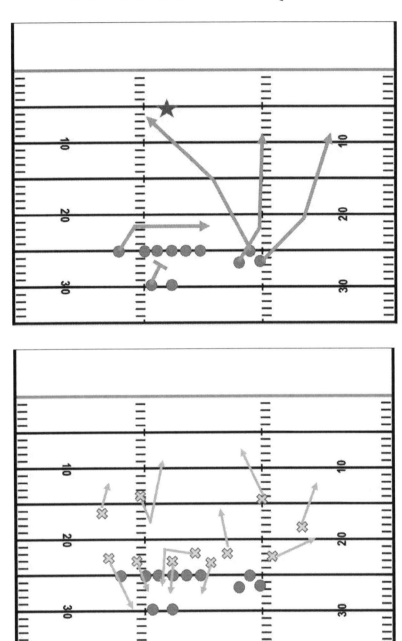

The Saints run a three man vertical concept out of a 3x1 bunch set. The bunch formation provides a clear advantage for the offense when using a vertical concept. The bunch prevents the defense from pressing every receiver and re-routing them.

The Chiefs call a fire zone blitz (5 man rush, 3 man underneath zone, and 3 deep zone). The Saints do a nice job of picking up the blitz, as the Saints bring 4 on the offense's left.

The short side safety has the flat zone on his side, but once he feels no threat, he retreats to help on the inside crossing route from the opposite side of the field. This forces a high throw from the QB that sails incomplete.

3rd & 1   Ball on own 34   3rd Quarter 14:09

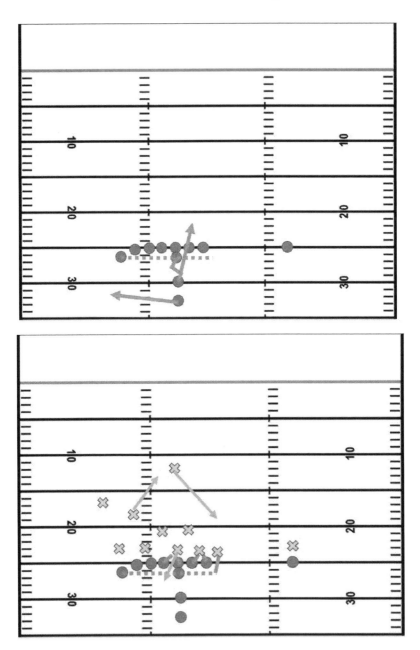

On 3rd and 1 the Saints use a quick-hitting fullback dive to pick up the first down. This play is a part of their short yardage package out of this formation. They will also fake the dive and toss the ball to the tailback going the opposite way.

The right guard and right tackle get an awesome double team on the 3 technique to create the surge that is needed.

The nose guard does a nice job of penetrating the opoosite A gap. Fortunately for the Saints, they had the dive called to the opposite side of the line.

3rd & 4   Ball on own 43   3rd Quarter 12:33

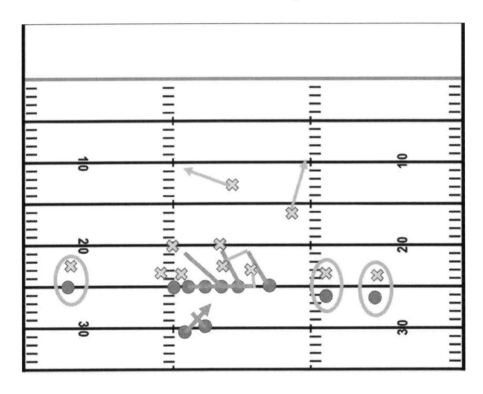

The Saints call a trap run out of trips on this third down. The Chiefs were expecting pass, and called a man under, two deep coverage.

The linebacker lined up just outside of the right guard backpedals when the ball is snapped in order to cover the tight end. The play side guard and tackle are both allowed to get to the next level because there are no penetrating down lineman on their side of the ball. This opens up a huge hole for the running back to pick up 15 yards and an easy first down.

When you watch the film of this play, check out the pancake block from the left guard. This is great teaching film for a pulling guard on trap blocks

3rd & 5   Ball on opponent 17   3rd Quarter 8:17

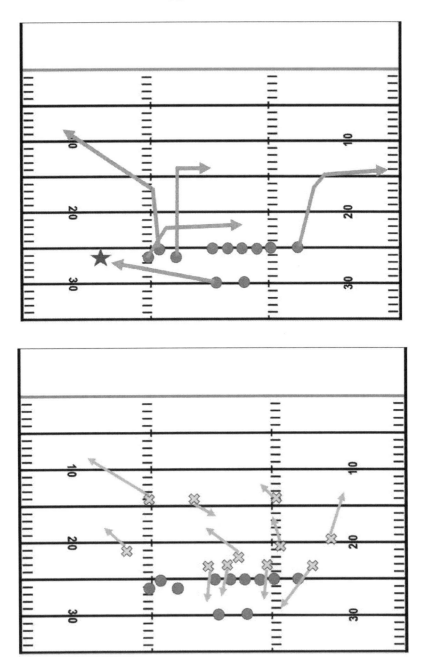

The Saints call the old west coast drive concept on their first third down in the red zone. The bunch formation gives each receiver a free release.

Progression Read:

1. Speed Out by #1 on right side
2. Drag
3. Dig
4. RB Swing

The Chiefs use a version of a Box/Solo coverage combination. The safety on the offense's right is keying the releases to the bunch side of the formation, and the defenders near the bunch match the releases of the routes after they separate from each other.

Brees cycles through his progression, but faces a little pressure when he gets to his dig read. This throws off his timing, and he is forced to check it down to the back swinging to the flat. The depth of the drag route also messes with his timing. The route is ran a couple of yards deeper than it should have, and this makes the window open later for the dig.

The Saints pick up the first down on a 7 yard completion.

3ʳᵈ & 7   Ball on own 39   3ʳᵈ Quarter 1:56

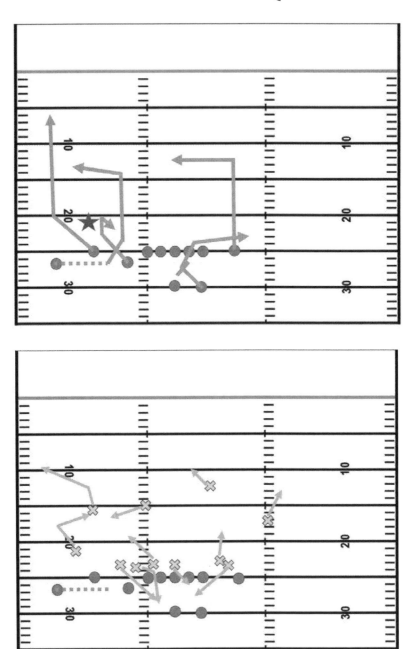

Progression Read:

1. Wheel
2. 10 Yard Out
3. Spot
4. Dig

The Saints call a variation of the three man flood concept. They use a spot route instead of the traditional flat route to attract the flat defender down. This variation is meant to look like the "H Post" concept they use out of the bunch formation, seen on page 76.

As the ball is being snapped, the Chiefs check to a box call against the bunch formation. This gives the Chiefs two outside defenders and two inside defenders to guard the three receivers. This check pays off, as the underneath outside defender sits into the window for the 10 yard out as the receiver makes his break, forcing the QB to look elsewhere.

The Chiefs do not react to the bait, and force the QB to check the ball to the spot route. The Chiefs make the tackle short of the first down marker, forcing a fourth down.

3rd & 8   Ball on opponent 25   4th Quarter 9:36

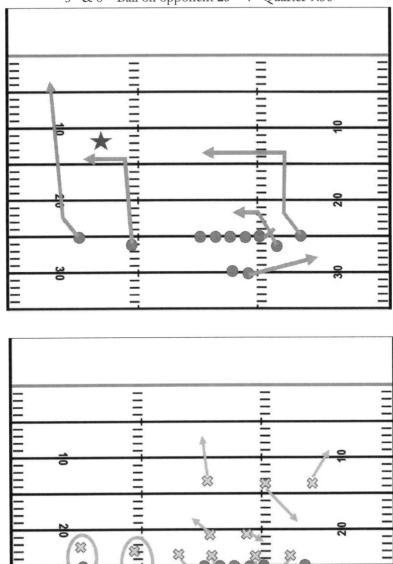

Progression Read

1. 10 Yard out
2. Dig
3. TE on chip release hitch route
4. RB on chip release swing route

The Saints used this same play on third down earlier in the game. The progression features two routes that will give the offense a first down if they are open. the chip block from the tight end and a check release from the running back will protect the quarterback's back side.

The Chiefs play press man to the offenses left, and a cover three spot drop on the offense's right.

The route technique from the slot recevier on the right is text book against man coverage. He releases to the side that gives him the best angle to break into his route. At the top of his stem, he leans into the defender. This creates the natural separation that creates the completion that gives the Saints the first down.

Robert J Peters & Richard Kusisto II

Week 8 vs Seattle

3rd & 4   Ball on 31   1st Quarter 13:51

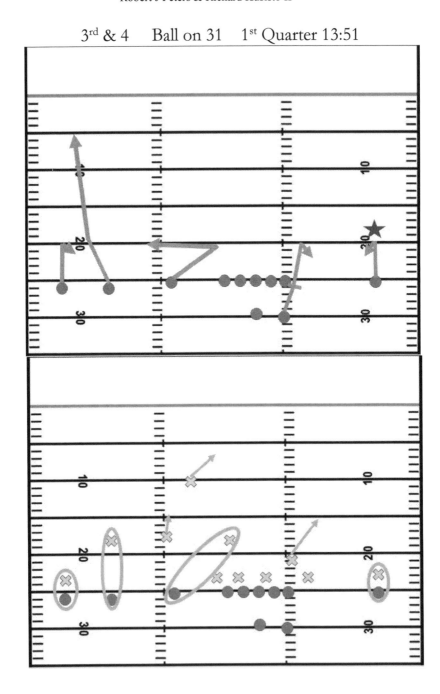

Coverage Read:

1. Vs single high coverage:
   a. Hitch
   b. RB Check Down
   c. Whip
2. Vs two high coverage
   a. Slot fade
   b. Whip Route
   c. RB Check Down

On the Saints first 3rd down of the game they come out with Trips to the left but they flex their TE to the farthest outside man. Offenses will do this to get an idea of what coverage the defense will be playing. If a CB bumps out to cover the TE then it is most likely zone but if a SS or LB ends up on him it is most likely man coverage.

A SS does line up on the TE and Brees knows he will have man coverage. Brees decides to take the 1 on 1 to the single receiver side and throws the hitch for an easy first down conversion.

As strange as this sounds, the Saints like to call a hitch vs a pressed corner (with a single high safety). With not much help over the top to defend the fade, a corner will bail hard against an outside release. This is the case on this play, and it gives the Saints a first down.

3rd & 9   Ball on own 39   1st Quarter 12:25

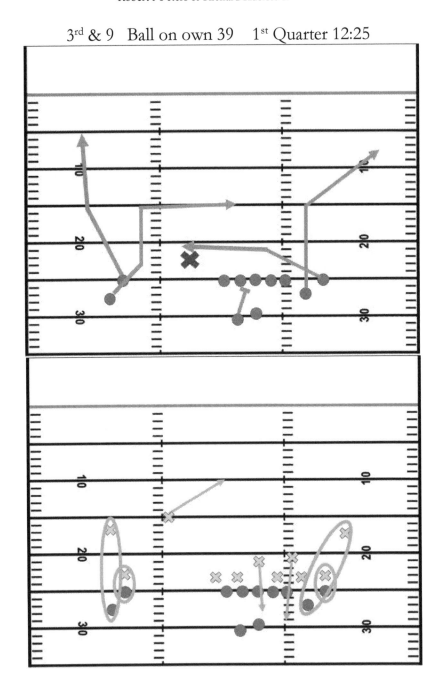

Progression Read:

1. Alert Corner Route
2. Wheel
3. Dig
4. Shallow

Faced with a 3rd and long, the Saints stack the receivers to the left and have a TE wing to the right with the receiver in a tight split. Seattle once again plays man coverage but this time brings some pressure along with it.

The Saints call a shallow crossing concept. This play will give an underneath checkdown against the Seahawks aggressive pattern matching rules. Brees keeps the RB in for protection to try and by himself a little extra time. Brees cycles through his progression and flings the ball to the shallow. With the defender in close pursuit, the ball falls incomplete.

3rd & 4   Ball on own 25   1st Quarter 6:33

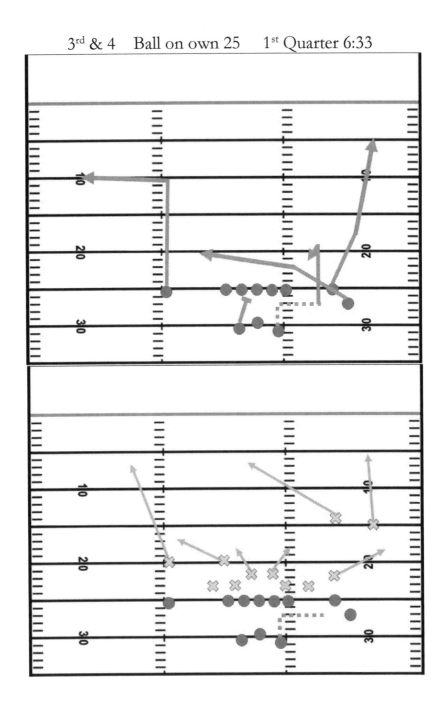

Progression Read:

1. Alert Wheel
2. Shallow
3. Spot

For this 3rd down, the Saints start with an RB to the left of Brees and a WR to his right. He then motions the WR out to the right where they now have a bunch formation. The Saints call a version of the H Post concept. On this version, the post route runner has the option to run a spot route if he finds himself in a void.

Seattle plays a spot dropping cover three, with the underneath defenders sitting at the first down line. The hook defender and flat defender bracket the spot route, giving Brees no option to throw to. Brees goes through his reads, tries to climb the pocket but the rush gets to him and he is sacked.

3rd & 3   Ball on own 20   1st Quarter 2:16

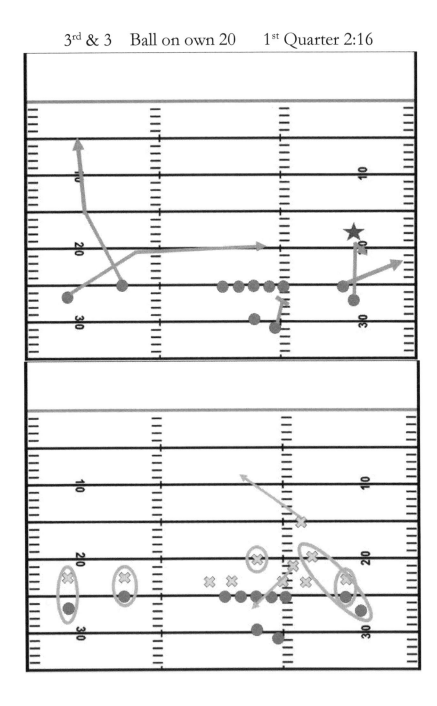

With the Saints facing a 3rd and short, they go to a widely used quick game play to get the conversion. With the 2 receivers stack to the right, the Saints run the "stick concept". In its most basic form, one receiver will run a flat route to 3 yards and the other receiver will hitch up at 5 yards. What the play does is put the LB in a bind, does he cover the flat or the hitch? Whichever he chooses, the offense will typically throw opposite.

Seattle happened to be playing man coverage again. The Saints snap the ball quickly, before the saftey has a chance to line up over the slot on the offense's right. Brees hits the stick route for a completion and a first down.

3rd & 1   Ball on own 49   1st Quarter :19

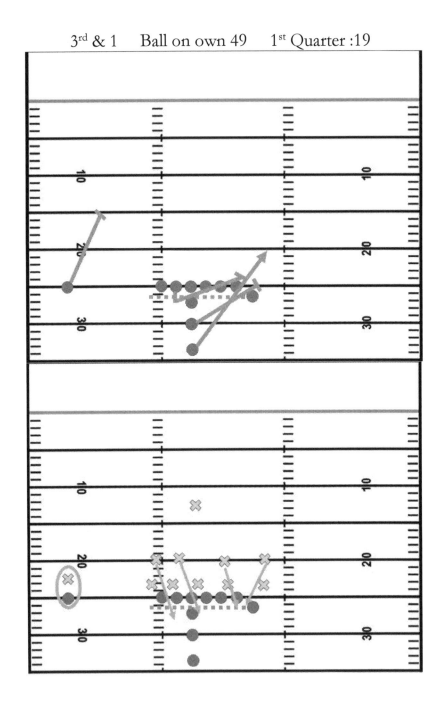

On third and short, the Saints turn to a base NFL play to keep the chains moving. Saints line up in an I formation with a TE and wing to the right and a single receiver to the left. They send the wing in motion to the other side of the formation with not much change in the defense. The Saints run to the Power play; a hard-nosed, "who wants it more" play.

The play side blocks down while the FB will kick out the end man on the line of scrimmage. The backside guard will pull through and aim for the inside backer to create a lane for the RB to run through. New Orleans gets great movement and easily picks up the first down.

3rd & 7   Ball on Seattle 10   2nd Quarter 12:20

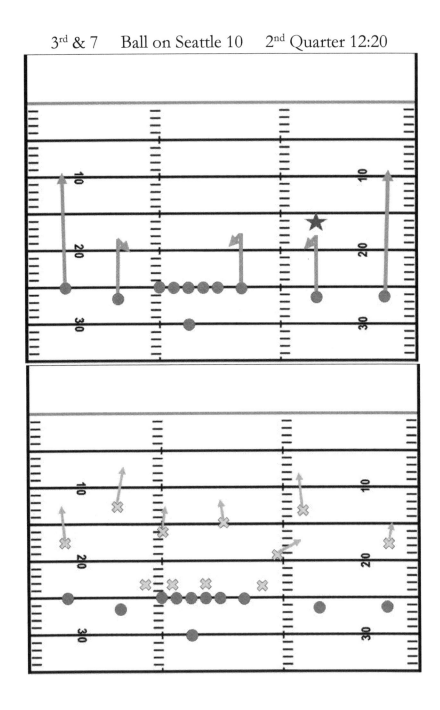

This 3rd down the Saints have trips to the right with the RB flexed out wide and 2 receivers to the left. Much like flexing the TE, flexing your RB out will help you to identify the coverage. Since the CB lines up across from him, the defense is in zone coverage.

The Saints call a spacing concept, anticipating a zone coverage or blitz. The Seahawks come out in a cover two, with all underneath defenders sitting on the first down marker.

The Outside linebacker on the right cheats in on the spot route from the #3 receiver. The Saints will typically hit the #3 on option routes against two high coverages.

Brees sees that this receiver is covered. and finds the #2 receiver sitting in space. The Saints get the comption, but get tackled short of the first down.

3rd & 3   Ball on Seattle 45   2nd Quarter 7:10

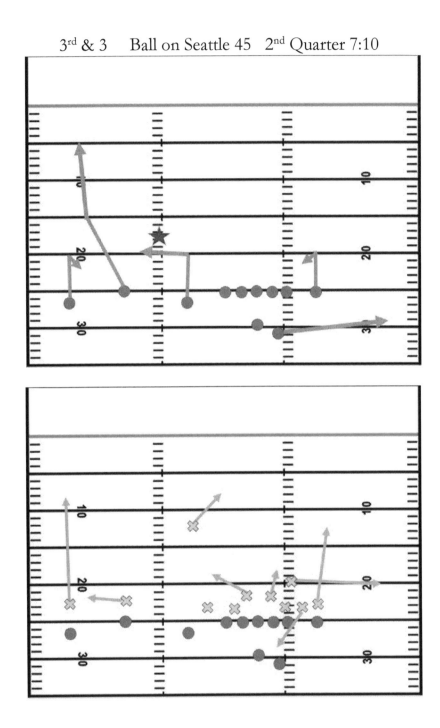

With 3rd and short in front of them, the Saints come out in trips to the left and a stand up TE to the right. They call a concept that has both man and zone beaters built in. Versus man, the fade from the slot would be best answer with the hitch and out being good zone beaters.

Seattle plays a soft zone and with the covering LB having to come all the way from the middle of the defense, it is an easy completion for a first down to the out route.

3ʳᵈ & 6   Ball on Seattle 35   2ⁿᵈ Quarter 5:26

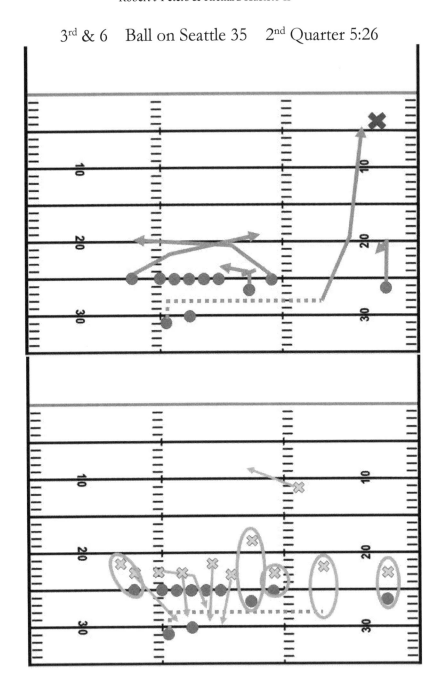

Progression Read:

1. Slot fade by RB
2. Hitch
3. Drag from Receiver on left
4. Chip Release Check Down

The Saint come out with trips to the right and a tight split by the TE to the left. Brees then motions the RB out to the right to give the Saints a quads look. The LB follows the RB as he motions out so Brees knows he has man coverage.

Brees detirmines pres-snap that if the saftey moves inside, he will throw the fade to the running back. Brees decides to take the RB/LB match up and the ball sails too far in front for an incompletion.

3rd & 2   Ball on Seattle 29   2nd Quarter 3:45

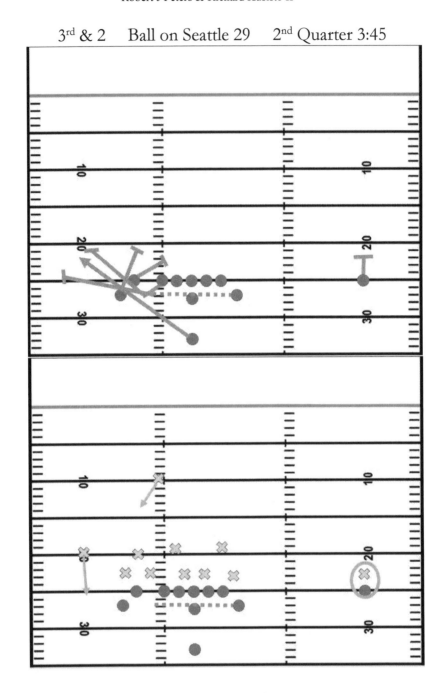

For this 3rd down, the Saints motion their wing TE to the left to get a bunch set and have a receiver split out wide to the right. The 2 receivers will block down to trap the defenders to the inside while the TE and tackle pull to the outside to lead block. With the CB being the force defender, he will be matched up with the TE and that is a battle an OC will take and the Saints easily convert for the 1st down.

3rd & 3   Ball on Seattle 4   2nd Quarter 2:00

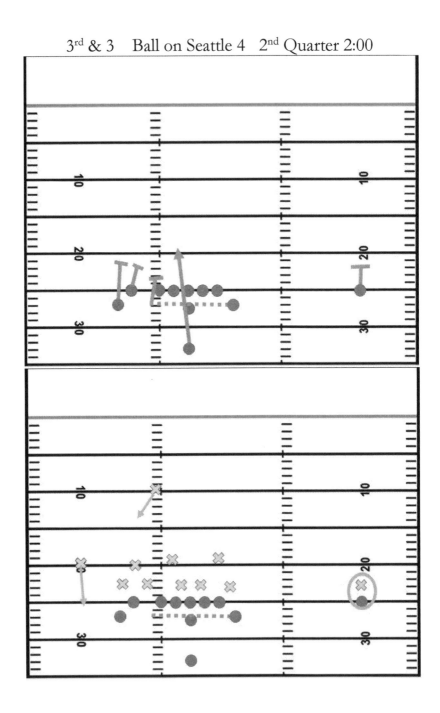

For this 3rd down the Saints come out in the exact same formation as their last 3rd down and even use the same motion. Except this time, they run right up middle for the 1st down. This is known as a constraint play, to make sure the defense doesn't over play to toss crack play the Saints ran earlier and to keep the defense guessing. The RB runs straight downhill as gets the 1st down.

3rd & Goal   Ball on Seattle 1   2nd Quarter :50

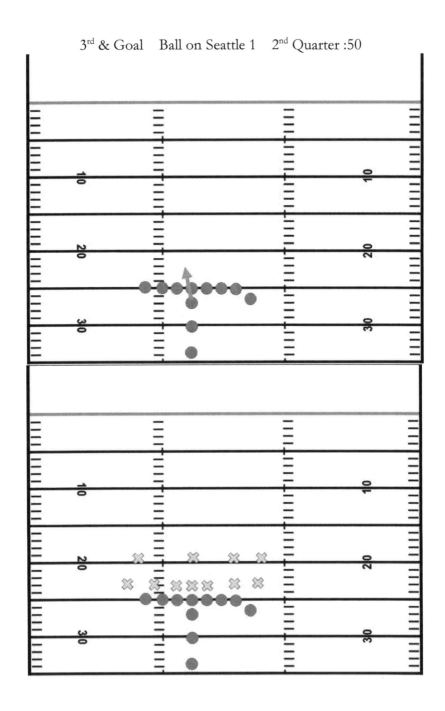

After 2 failed run attempts on the 1 yard line, the Saints are faced with a 3rd & 1. They decide to go with the QB sneak. What is puzzling is that Seattle has their LB's 5 yards deep in the end zone. The Saints then O-line to submarines down and Brees goes over the top for an easy Touchdown.

3rd & Goal   Ball on Seattle 1   3rd Quarter 4:01

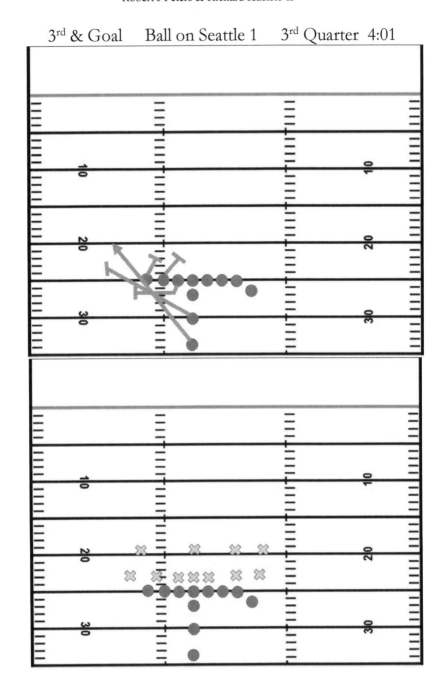

The Saints face another 3rd and goal from the 1 and come out in the standard goal line formation. This time they run G-lead weak, or for your wing-t guys out there, Belly. This play is normally run to a 3 tech with the tackle and TE blocking down. The guard then pulls and kicks out the end man on the line of scrimmage with the FB leading through. The backside guard unfortunately misses his block and the DT makes the play in the back field to stop the Saints short.

3ʳᵈ & Goal   Ball on Seattle 2   4ᵗʰ Quarter 12:30

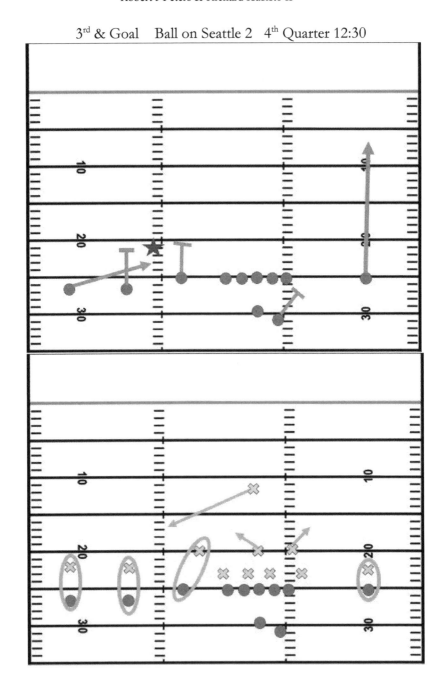

The Saints once again find themselves in a 3rd and goal situation. This time they decide to spread the formation out with trips to the left and a single receiver to the right. The Saints run the outside receiver to the left on a quick slant with the 2 inside receivers "getting in the way" of the defenders over them. This play is great against man coverage and Seattle indeed does play man. The receiver is able to get enough separation from his defender for the completion and touchdown.

3rd & 4   Ball on Seattle 44   4th Quarter 3:55

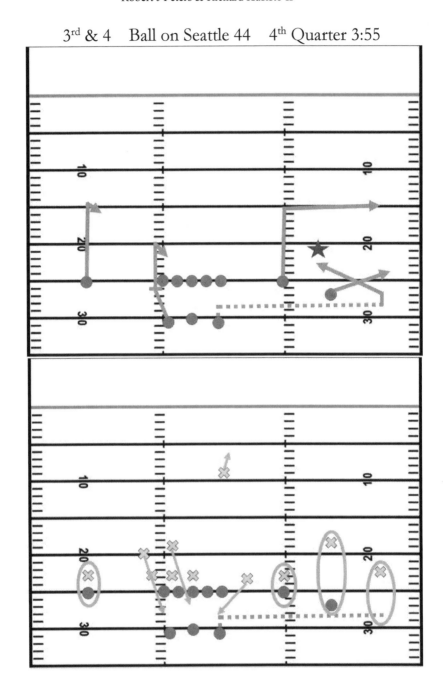

Facing a 3rd and medium, the Saints line up with a FB to Brees left and a WR to his right. Brees motions the WR out to the far right of the formation with the nickel safety following him. This is one of the benefits and strategy of lining a WR up in the backfield to start a play. You are trying to see if you can get a mismatch in personnel with a lesser defender across from a speedy and shifty receiver. The offense runs a similar play to their last 3rd play with the outside receiver running a quick slant and the inside receiver getting in the way of the defenders. The receiver breaks free and Brees tosses an easy 1st down completion.

3rd & 10   Ball on Seattle 10   4th Quarter 2:22

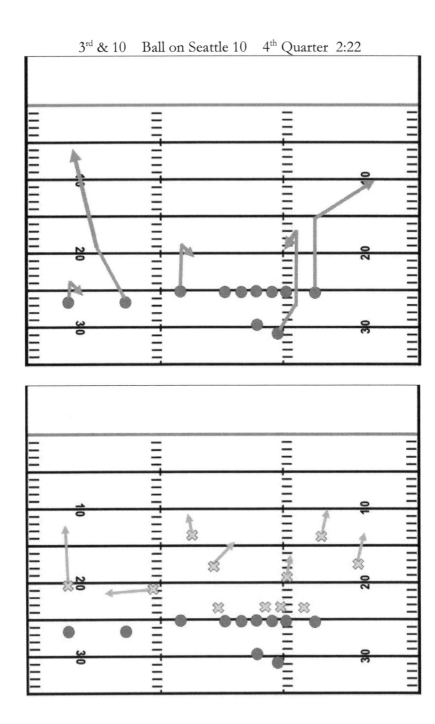

With a 3rd and long in front of them, the Saints come back to one of their favorite plays with the slot seam and 2 hitches. With the Saints being so close to the goal line, the outside hitch is just one step to give the fade more room.

Seattle only rushes 4 and drops everyone else into coverage. Brees cycles through his progression, and when he gets to the back out of the backfield, he finds pressure in his face. The right guard was not able to pick up the stunt on his side. The coverage down field is conservative, and the rush eventually gets to Bees and he is brought down to the turf for a 3rd down sack.

Week 9 at San Francisco

3rd & 12   Ball on 31   1st Quarter 12:36

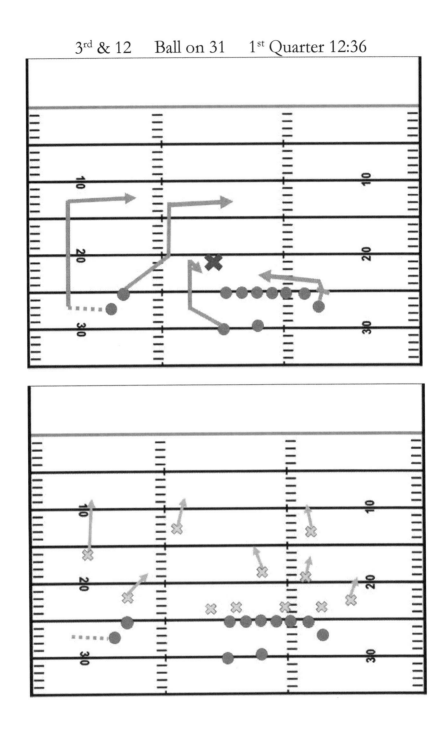

Progression Read:
1. Inside Dig
2. Outside Dig
3. Spot route
4. TE chip release shallow

Faced with a 3rd and long the Saints line up with 2 receivers to the left in a stack, a TE to the right and a WR in the backfield. Brees motions the outside receiver in the stack out just before snapping the ball.

The Saints are trying to read the Safety on the left hash and use his decision against him. If the safety bites on the inside dig, Brees will throw the outside dig. If the safety takes away the outside dig, Brees will then hit the inside dig.

On the snap, the safety opens toward the outside dig but the defense has the Mike LB drop into the deep middle and he takes away the inside dig throw. Brees is then forced to take the spot route but he ball is knocked to the turf by the defense.

3rd & 5 Ball on own 22 Quarter 1 8:44

Coverage Read

1. Vs single high safety: Read combination on the right

2. Vs two high safeties: Read combination on the left

For this 3rd down, the Saints flex their TE out wide to the right with the SS following indicating man coverage. With this alignment, the CB follows the WR to the slot, which puts the CB in a position he isn't use to with all the space to the outside. Brees likes this match up and throws a great back shoulder to the inside fade route for a big gain and a 1st down.

3rd & 2   Ball on San Francisco 47   1st Quarter 7:35

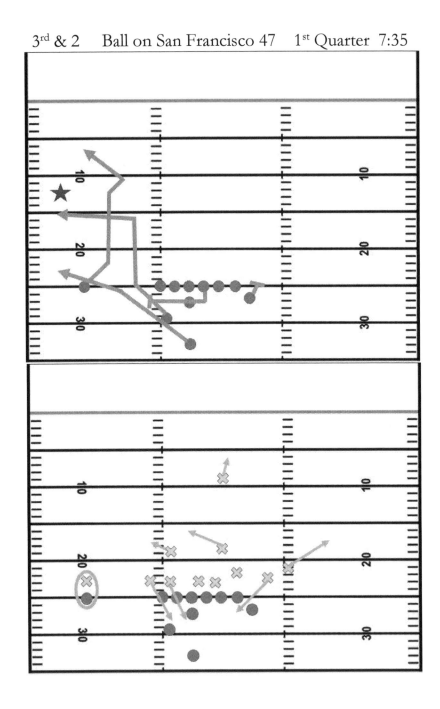

Progression Read

1. Post-Corner

2. FB on 10 yard out

3. TB in flat

For this 3rd and short, the Saints come out in a heavy run formation and use the defenses aggressiveness against them. The offense fakes power to the left with the pulling backside guard and the fake hand off to the running back. The single receiver runs a post corner, taking the CB and the FS with him. The play fake sucks both inside linebackers up and the TE who was actually lined up in the full back position is wide open for the easy completion and the 1st down.

3rd & 9 Ball on San Francisco 13 Quarter 1 5:58

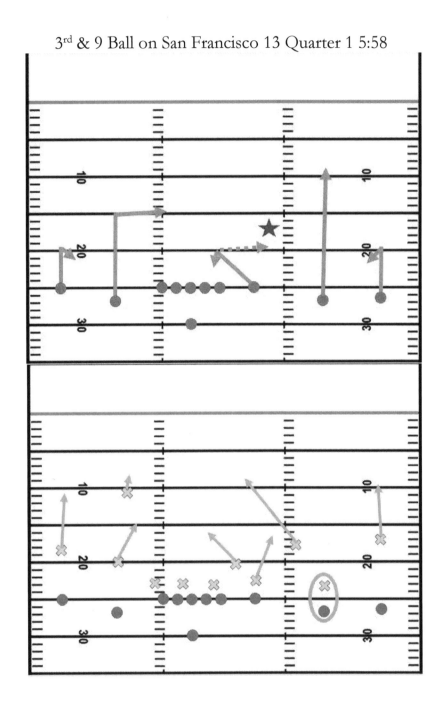

Combination Read

1. Vs single high safety
   a. Seam (#2 on right)
   b. Hitch (#1 on right)

2. Vs two high safeties
   a. Spot route (#3 on right)
   b. Dig (#2 on left)
   c. Hitch-Drive (#1 on left)

Facing a 3rd and long, the Saints empty the backfield and place the RB out to the far right.

The 49ers drop into a 4 deep zone with the LB over the TE fighting to cut off the seam. This places the inside backer essentially 1 on 1 with the TE. The TE sits down then, works to the sideline to find the open grass as Brees hits him in stride for the 1st down.

3rd & Goal   Ball on San Francisco 1   1st Quarter 2:17

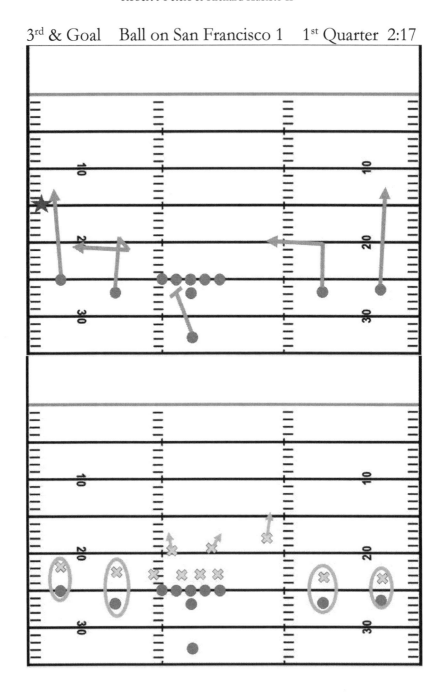

Pre-snap read based on matchups and leverage.

With 3rd and Goal from the 1, the Saints put 2 WR on each side of the formation to spread the defense out. To no surprise the defense plays man coverage and Brees takes the 1 on 1 match on the outside to the left. Brees throws a beautiful back shoulder throw for the conversion and touchdown.

3rd & 2   Ball on San Francisco 23   2nd Quarter 9:02

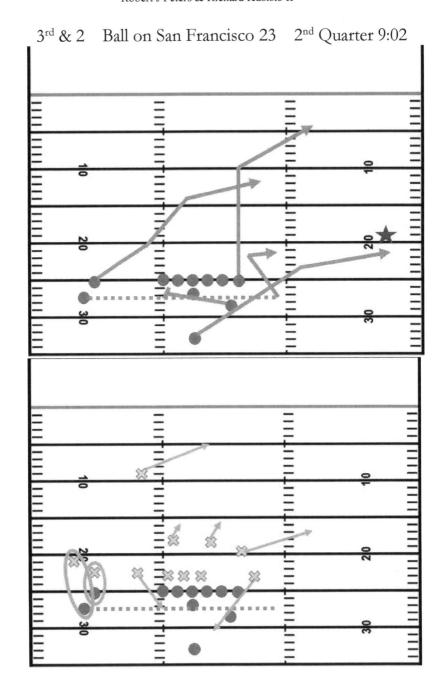

Progression Read:

1. TB in flat
2. Corner Route
3. Whip route from motion man
4. Deep cross

Facing another 3rd and short, the Saints once again use motion and play action to get the defense out of position. From the stacked receivers on the left, Brees motions the outside receiver to the other side of the formation and the CB follows him step for step.

At the snap, the whole offensive line slides to the left along with the FB as Brees opens up that way for a play fake. While that is happening, the RB release immediately to the flat on the right and out flanks the flat defender to that side. Brees sets up after the play fake and finds his RB in the flat for the 1st down.

3rd & Goal   Ball on Opponent 5   2nd Quarter 7:46

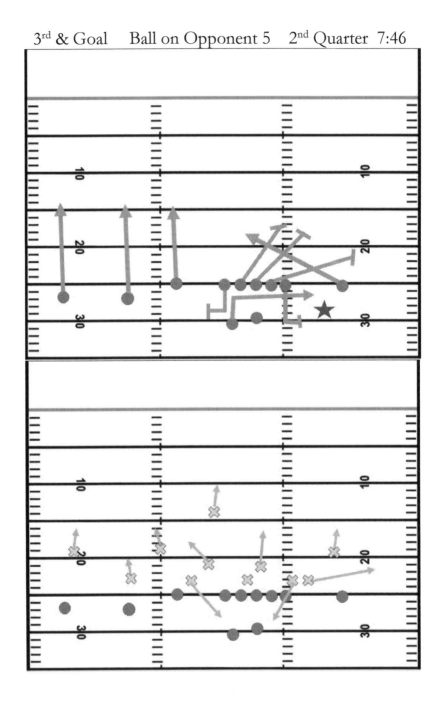

With a 3rd and Goal in front of them, the Saints put 3 WR to the left and a single WR to the right. The Saints call a RB screen pass and the dropping LB to the flat does a great job of forcing the play back inside. The RB however makes to great moves, making defenders miss as he spins his way into the end zone for a touchdown.

3rd & 4   Ball on own 46   2nd Quarter 2:00

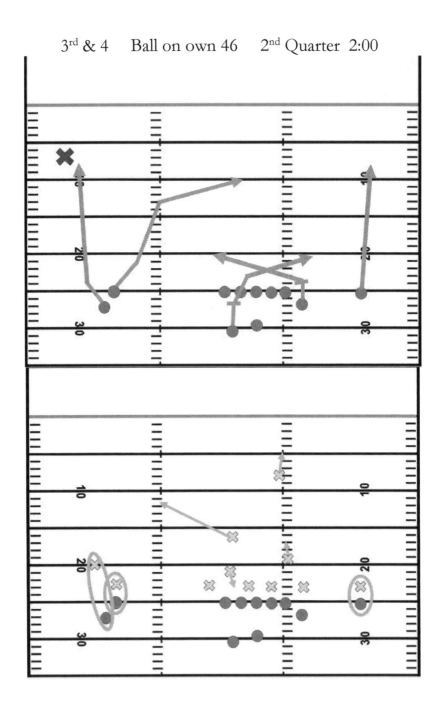

Progression Read

1. Peak Fade
2. Deep Cross
3. Chip-release check downs

With a 3rd and medium in front of them, the Saints go to a version of Y-cross to try and get the conversion. With 2 receivers stacked to the left, the inside WR runs the cross as the outside WR runs a fade. With 1 on 1 coverage, the outside WR has nothing but grass to the outside of him while the CB is in trail. Unfortunately, Brees short arms the throw allowing the CB to catch up and bat the ball away.

3rd & 7   Ball on own 4   3rd Quarter 10:56

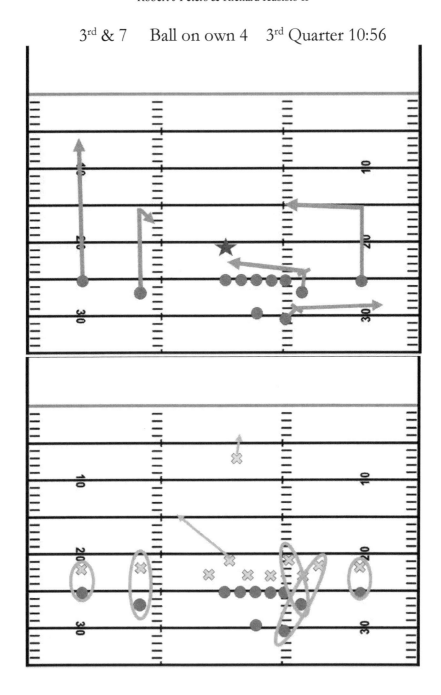

Progression read:

1.Fade

2. 10 Yard curl

3. TE chip release shallow

4. 10 yard Dig

With a 3rd and long, the Saints find themselves back up deep in their own territory. The call a version of the drive concept, which will give them access to completions that will give them a first down.

The 49ers play man coverage across the board and with good coverage across the board, Brees is forced to dumped the ball off to the TE shallow. With the SS in close pursuit, he makes the tackle to bring up 4th down.

3rd & 8   Ball on own 42   3rd Quarter 7:02

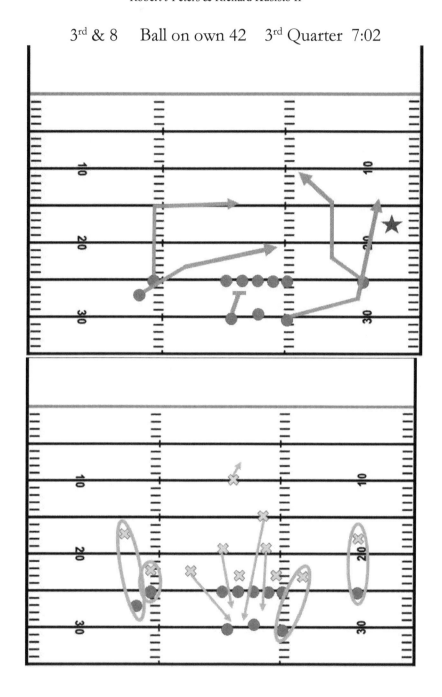

Progression read:

1.Post
2. Wheel
3. Shallow
4. Dig

For this 3rd down, the Saints get a little creative and set one of their slot receivers to the right of Brees in the backfield and stack 2 receivers to the left. Teams like to put WR in the backfield in an attempt to get them matched up on a slower SS or LB.

At the snap, the defense brings pressure and defaults to playing man coverage. As the WR from the backfield releases, the outside LB follows him and Brees has the match up he wanted. With the LB hustling not to get beat deep, Brees is able to put the ball slightly behind the WR and convert the 3rd down to get the drive alive.

3ʳᵈ & 2   Ball on San Francisco 41   3ʳᵈ Quarter 5:24

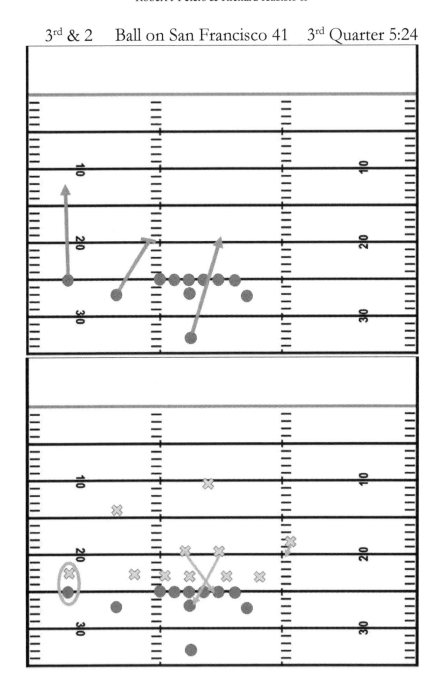

For this 3rd and short, the offense doesn't do anything too special and just runs an off tackle run to the strong side. The two inside LB's do an X blitz making the blocks even easier for the offensive line. The line is able to get great push and easily pick up the first down.

3rd & 11 Ball on San Francisco 37 3rd Quarter 3:06

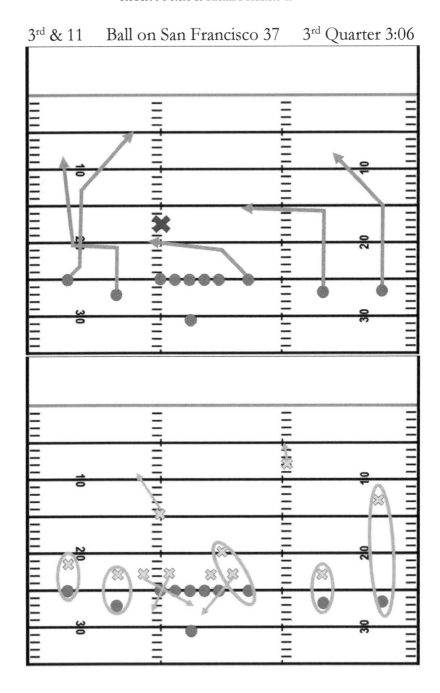

Progression Read:
1. Alert: RB post (right side)
2. Post on the left
3. Wheel
4. Shallow
5. Dig

With a 3rd and long in front of them, the Saints once again empty the backfield by placing their RB out to the far right. The LB follows the RB out, confirming the defense is playing some sort of man coverage.

At the snap, the safety plays over the top of both the post and wheel routes forcing Brees to come off to this 3 read. The LB is in close pursuit of the TE shallow and knocks the ball lose for an incompletion.

3rd & 4   Ball on own 29   3rd Quarter 0:30

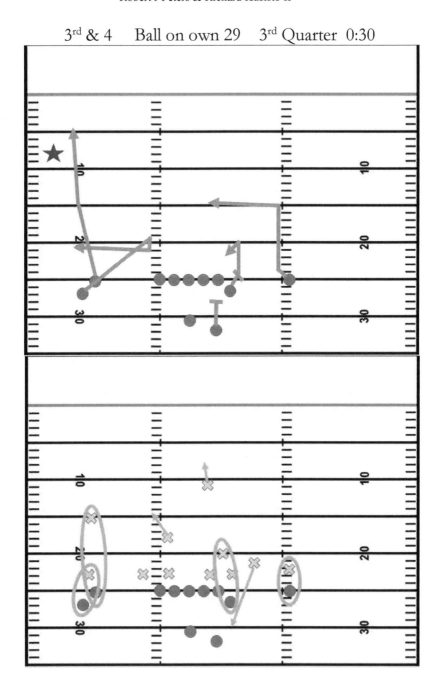

Progression Read:

1. Fade
2. Whip
3. Dig
4. Chip-release hitch

Faced with a 3rd and 4, the Saints stack the WR to the left and run a rub combination. The Saints have been getting man coverage from the defense in most 3rd downs, so the play call is based off that.

The defender over the point of the stack runs with the whip route, leaving some open space for the fade to the sideline. Brees throws a nice back shoulder ball and the Saints convert the 3rd down.

3rd & 1   Ball on San Francisco 34   4th Quarter 13:58

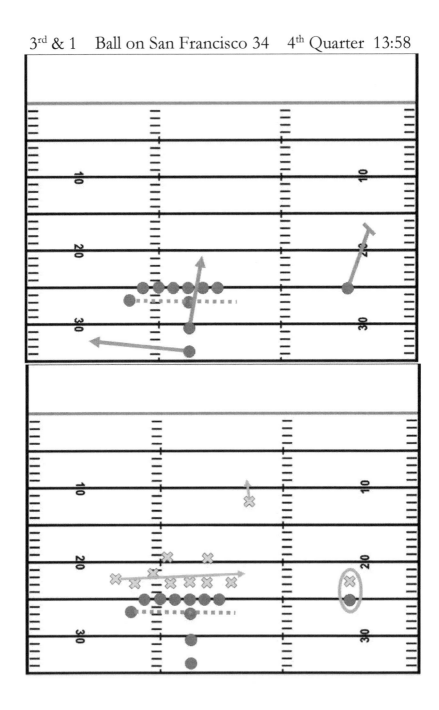

With a 3rd and short in front of them, the Saints go to the FB dive. The offensive line fires off the ball and creates enough movement to push the defense back and convert the 3rd down.

3rd & 6   Ball on San Francisco 42   4th Quarter 10:32

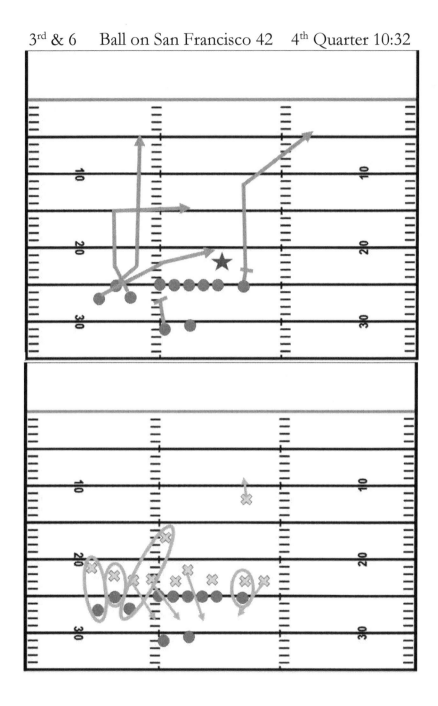

Progression Read:

1. Corner
2. Drag
3. Dig

With a 3rd down and 6 in front of them, the Saints bunch their WR to the left and stand up the TE to the right. The point man of the bunch runs a seam route to clear out the middle of the defense, he is the decoy man. The Saints then run a Dig/Shallow combo underneath him with Brees reading Shallow to Dig.

The defense plays man coverage and the CB playing the shallow runner in set outside the bunch, putting in a disadvantage from the beginning. The shallow runner is able to get a step on the CB and Brees throws a nice easy pass to keep marching down the field.

3rd & 5   Ball on San Francisco 23   4th Quarter 9:00

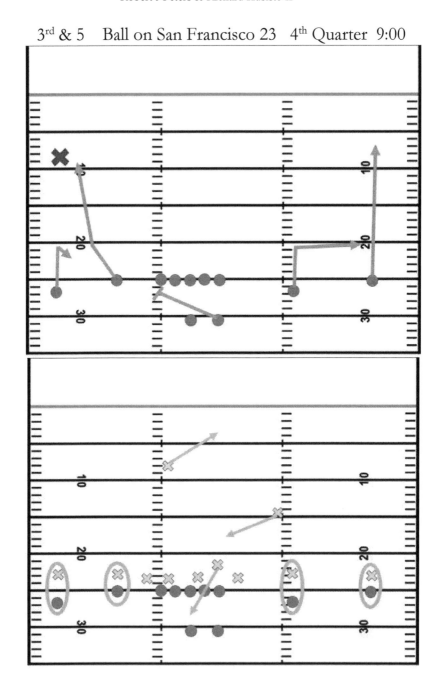

Coverage Read:

1. Vs single high safety (& man): combination on the left
2. Vs two high safeties: combination on the right

Facing a 3rd and medium, the Saints go to one of their favorite plays. The Saints flex out their TE to the far left and have a twins look to each side. To the right side, the offense runs a zone beating concept while the concept to the left is a good man beater.

The defense plays man coverage with 2 high safeties. The 2 safeties end up rolling to a robber look and in doing so take themselves out of the play. Brees takes his shot to the slot fade. The WR and QB seem to be on different pages as Brees tosses a back shoulder and the WR tries to beat the defender deep and the pass falls incomplete.

Robert J Peters & Richard Kusisto II

Week 10 vs Denver

3rd & 9   Ball on opponent 49   1st Quarter 13:11

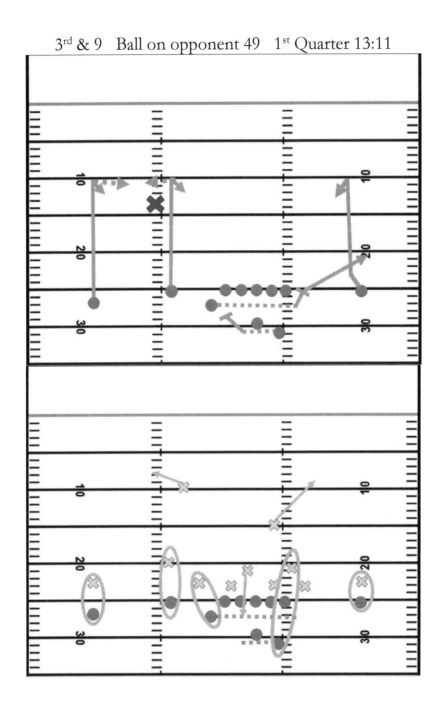

Facing a 3rd and long, the Saints come out with trips the left with the TE in a wing alignment and a single WR split to the right. Brees calls a dummy snap count the flips both the TE and RB to opposite where they lined up. The defenders over both the plays follow them step for step confirming that the defense is in man coverage. The 2 WR to the left run 15 yard curls and in an attempt to find open grass they end up working right into each other. The defense is able to make a play on the ball and knock it down for an incompletion.

3rd & 5   Ball on own 30   1st Quarter 4:57

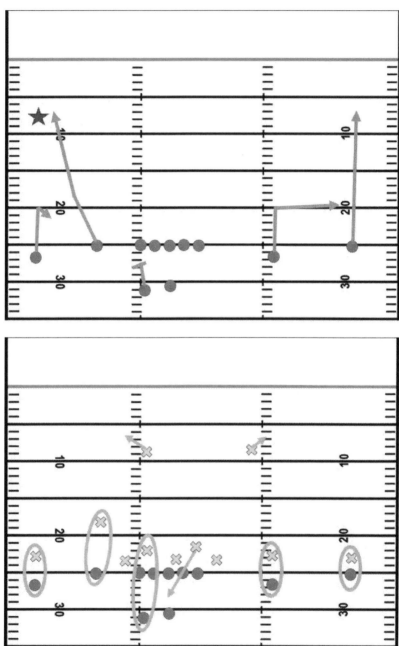

Coverage Read

1. Vs single high safety:

    a. Vs man: combination on left

    b. Vs zone: speed out on the right

2. Vs two high safeties: Pick a side based on safeties' pre-snap leverage

With a 3rd and medium in front of them, the Saints come out with 2 WR to each side of the formation. They go to one of their favorite quick game concepts on this 3rd down with the hitch/slot fade to the left and flat/fade to the right. It is important to get rid of the ball quick for each of these concepts, as the safeties become more of a factor the longer the play takes. These quick game combinations are all about matchup's and pre-snap determinations.

With the defense showing man coverage Brees likes his slot fade to the left and takes the throw there. Brees throws a perfect ball, dropping it in to his WR for the 1st down.

3ʳᵈ & 2   Ball on Denver 24   1ˢᵗ Quarter 2:34

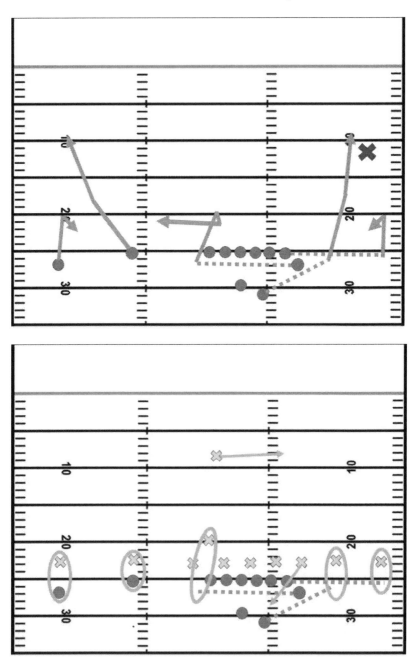

Coverage Read:

1. Vs two high safeties: whip route isolated on middle linebacker

2. Vs single high safety: Pick a side and read slot fade - hitch

For this 3rd down, the Saints do a bunch of pre snap movement to try and get the defense out of position and to gain a match up advantage. The Saints start with motioning the wing TE to the left and let him get set. The Saints then flex out their other TE to the far right and have the RB motion out in the slot to the right.

The Saints get a SS over the TE and a CB over the RB. Brees likes his match up with the RB and takes his shot there. Unfortunately for Brees, the Safety sees the play the whole way and flies over to that side for the interception.

3rd & 3   Ball on own 32   2nd Quarter 12:52

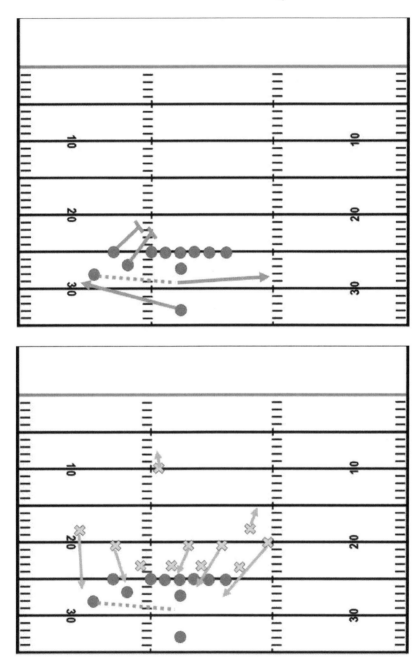

For a 3rd and short, the Saints line up in a bunch to the left with an attached TE to the right. They send the outside receiver in motion as if he were going to take a hand off on a jet sweep. But the Saints have no intention on running the sweep as the whole offensive line fires off to the left. The 2 WR to the left both crack block down as Brees tosses the ball to the RB going left. The RB is able to out run the defense for the conversion to keep the drive going.

3rd & 7   Ball on own 49   2nd Quarter 10:55

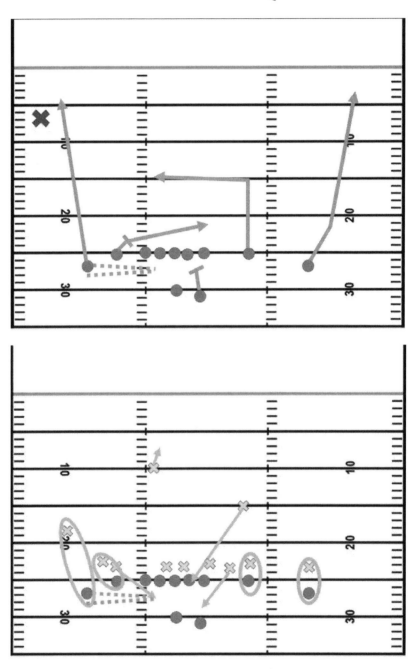

Progression Read:

1. Fade to the left

2. Dig

3. Chip Release Drag

For this 3rd and long, the Saints compress their formation on the left. They send the outside WR to the left in a return motion and the CB follows him the whole way indicating man coverage. The motion also gives the WR outside leverage for the fade throw.

Brees decides to take his shot to the outside fade to the left but the ball is slightly over thrown and falls incomplete.

3rd & 1   Ball on own 23   2nd Quarter 4:09

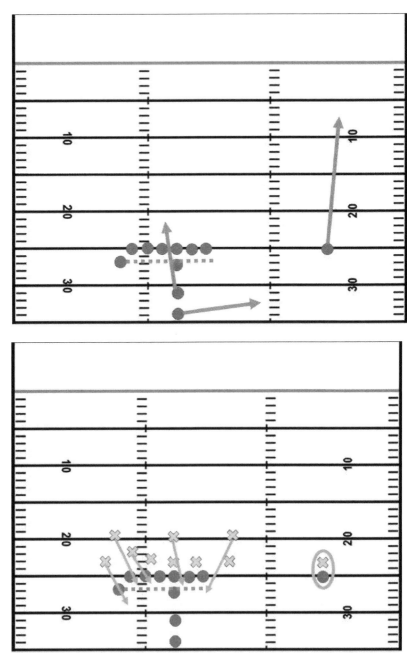

On this third and short, the Saints go to one of their favorite short yardage packages, FB dive with a flip toss to the tailback going opposite. This time Brees fakes the FB dive and tosses the ball out to the RB. The defense has great pursuit and is able to tackle the RB before he gets to the 1st down.

3rd & 4   Ball on own 16   3rd Quarter 11:10

Progression Read:

1. Alert: Fade

2. Corner

3. Shallow

4. Dig

5. RB check swing

For this 3rd down the Saints once again compress the formation with 3 WR bunched to the right and a stand up TE to the left. As with most 3rd downs so far in this game, the defense once again plays man coverage. Brees cycles through his read to his 3rd, the dig. The LB is dropping into the deep middle put Brees puts the ball just outside of his reach and completes the pass for the 1st down.

3rd & 5   Ball on own 30   4th Quarter 8:31

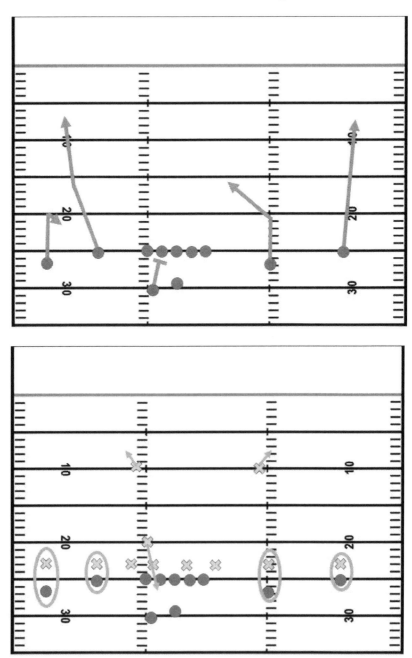

Coverage Read:

1. Vs single high safety: read combination on left

2. Vs two high safeties, read combination on right. Throw off of the right safeties hips

With a 3rd and medium in front of them, the Saints decide to run one of their favorite concepts, the hitch/slot fade. The play call is a good one as the defense is in man coverage and the slot fade is designed to beat man. The defense however, plays 2 safeties high to roam the deep halves and the safety is able to take away the slot fade. Brees attempts to step up in the pocket but the rush gets to him and he is sacked on the play.

3rd & 2 Ball on Denver 38 Quarter 4 2:00

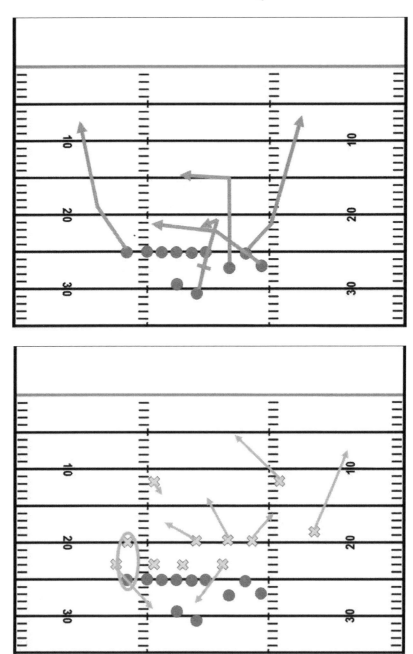

Progression Read:

1. Alert: Fade on the right

2. TE fade on the left

3. Shallow

4. Dig

5. RB check sit route

Facing a 3rd and short, the Saints line up with 3 WR to the right in a bunch formation and a stand up TE to the left. The Saints run a drive concept out of the bunch, which is a popular play to run out of bunch. The WR at the point runs a fade to essentially take the top off the defense and open up underneath. The other 2 WR will run a dig and a shallow route.

The defense ends up playing zone to the bunch side and takes away all of Brees options. However, the dropping LB's forget about the RB as he check releases underneath them, and is wide open. Brees finds his RB and dumps the ball down for the 1st down.

Week 11 at Carolina

3rd & 8   Ball on own 39   1st Quarter 13:23

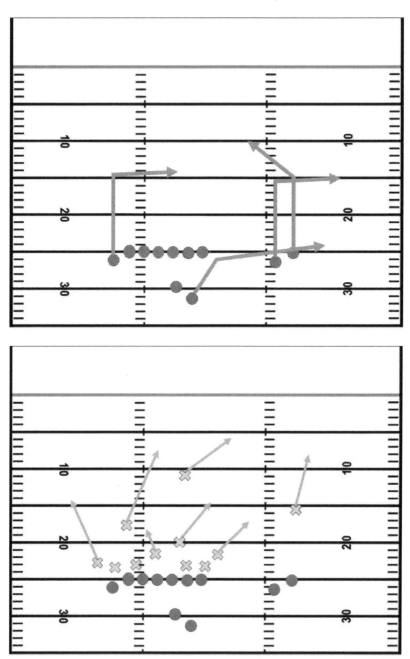

Progression Read:

1. Post
2. 10 Yard Out
3. RB Flat
4. Dig

The Saints call a variation of the flood concept on their first third down of the day. The post route is meant to take advantage of any open grass on the right side of the field, Which would give the Saints an easy way to get a big play.

The Panthers rush four, and roll their coverage to the two receiver side. The coverage ends up looking like cover two.

Brees cylces through his entire progression. He chooses not to take the running back, who is open in the flat. Instead, he resets his feet to the dig. Once he realizes the dig is covered, he gets sacked. He had plenty of time on the play, as he was able to look at each receiver.

3rd & 1   Ball on Carolina 36   1st Quarter 5:04

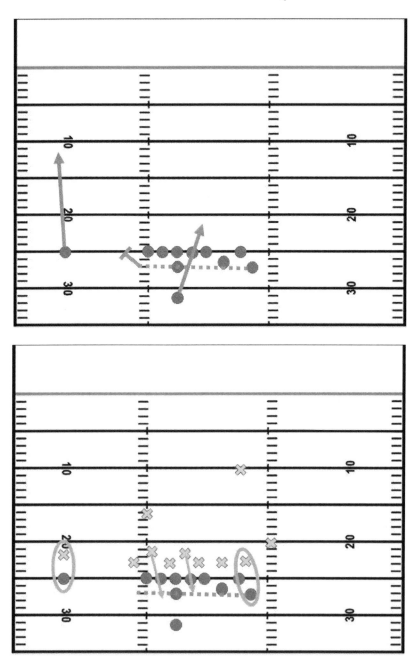

On third and short, the Saints use a quick motion, with a quick snap, to hand the ball to the fullback.

The Panthers have a down lineman to cover each gap on the play side. The Saints offensive line gets a nice push, and washes each defender inside. The fullback is able to find a crease to pick up two yards and a Saints first down.

3rd & 8 Ball on Carolina 32 1st Quarter 3:14

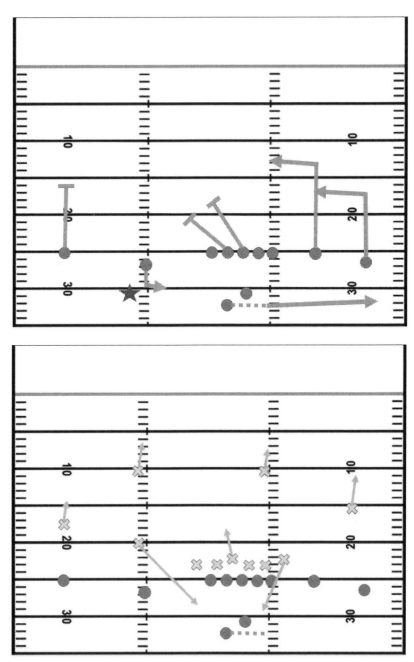

The Saints were well prepared for this third down. They had the perfect play call on for what the Panthers did defensively.

With the nickel blitz coming off of the slot on the right, the quick screen has quite a bit of green grass to work with. The left guard releases to get a body on the safety. The receiver does a nice job of setting this block up, and cutting inside off of it. This play can be great film for teaching a receiver how to set up blocks on a screen.

The Saints pick up fifteen yards, and a first down.

3ʳᵈ & 2   Ball on Carolina 10   1ˢᵗ Quarter 1:04

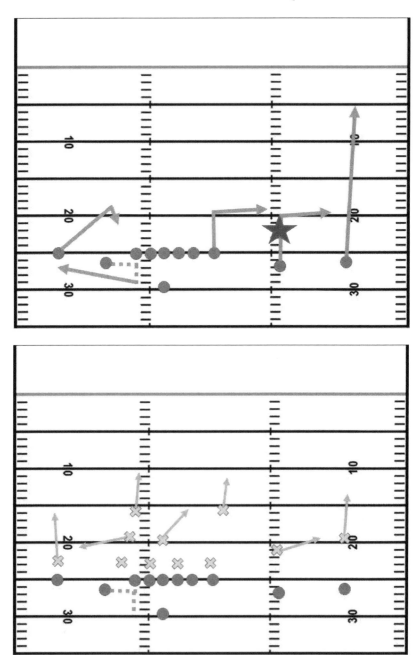

Coverage Read:

1. Based on pre-snap leverage, determine if stick (right side) will be open. Typically vs two high safeties.

2. If not, then read snag to swing on the left.

This play is a great example of how to use motion to the offense's advantage. The action from the slot motioning to the backfield distracts the linebacker, and gets him to jump the swing route.

The Panthers rush four, and play soft to the trips side. Once again, the Saints have a great play call for this specific defense. The stick combination takes advantage of the space afforded in the slot, and the Saints pick up the first down.

3ʳᵈ & 6   Ball on own 23   2ⁿᵈ Quarter 11:47

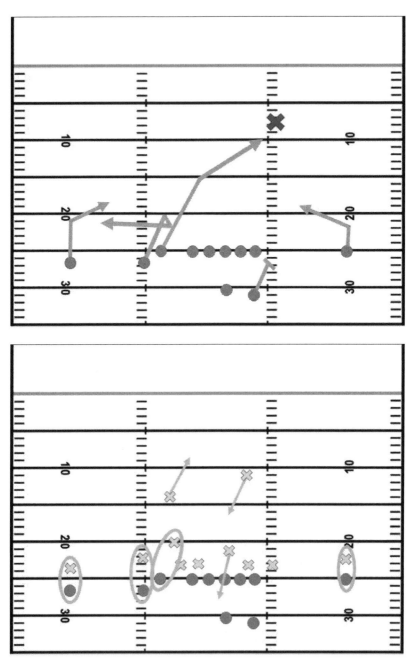

Once Brees identifies the Panthers are playing man coverage right after the ball is snapped. He then locates his best matchup, the tight end matched up on the middle linebacker on the deep crossing route.

The Panthers rush four, and play a cover 1 robber. Brees feels some pressure from the inside, and throws the deep cross off his back foot. This causes the ball to sail, and brings up a fourth down.

3rd & 1   Ball on own 10   2nd Quarter 4:22

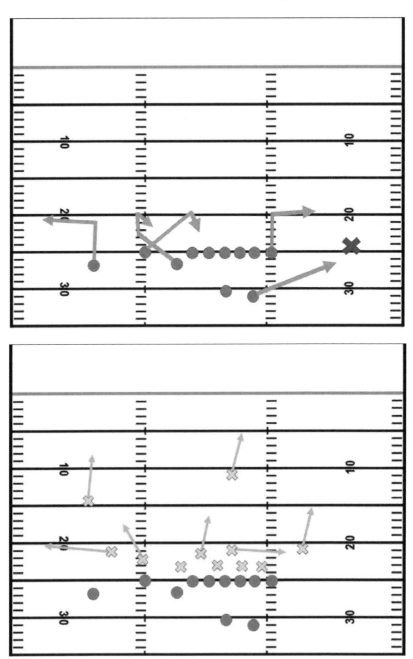

Coverage Read:

1. Vs single high safety: Read stick to swing on right. Spot route over the middle will be the check down.

2. Vs two high safeties: read outside – in on concept to the left.

The Saints turn to another quick game concept on this third and short. On the last third and short, the Saints got a soft coverage from the Panthers, and are hoping for another one here.

The Panthers play a soft cover 3, exactly what the Saints were hoping for. The stick route rubs the flat defender, giving the flat route leverage on the right. Brees throws the route, but the ball gets deflected at the line of scrimmage, bringing up fourth down.

3rd & 10   Ball on Carolina 20   2nd Quarter 0:42

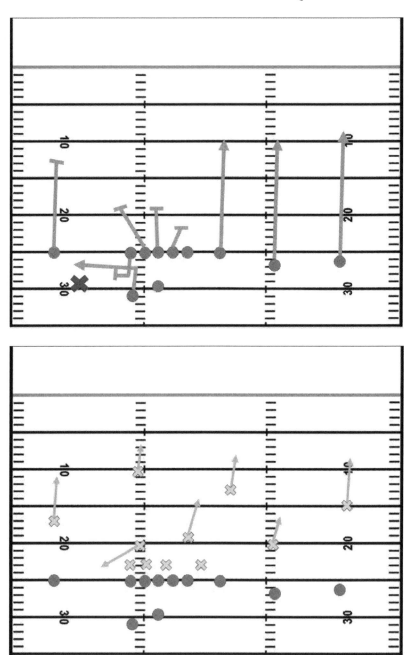

This third down takes place during a two minute drill at the end of the half. The Saints set up a running back screen away from the trips.

There seems to be a miscommunication, as the offensive line does not pull to block the screen. Brees is forced to throw it away, bringing up a fourth down.

3rd & 9   Ball on Carolina 43   3rd Quarter 6:31

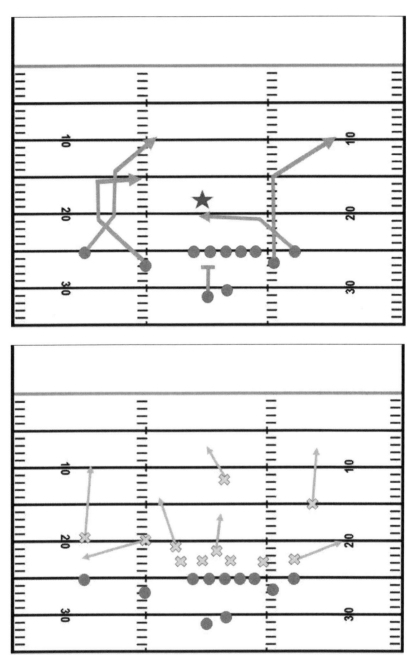

Progression Read:

1. Corner
2. Post
3. Drag
4. Dig

The Saints use a switch release on this shallow cross concept. The switch releases are a good way to disrupt any pattern match rules.

The Panthers play a soft cover three, and rush four. The post route is taken away by the safety rotating over, reading the quarterback's eyes. The dig is taken away by the hook defender on the offense's left. This leaves a small void for the drag route to sit down in.

The soft zone does its job on this third down. Brees hits the drag route, and the Panthers rally to make the tackle a few yards shy of a first down.

3rd & 4 Ball on Carolina 17 Quarter 3 2:57

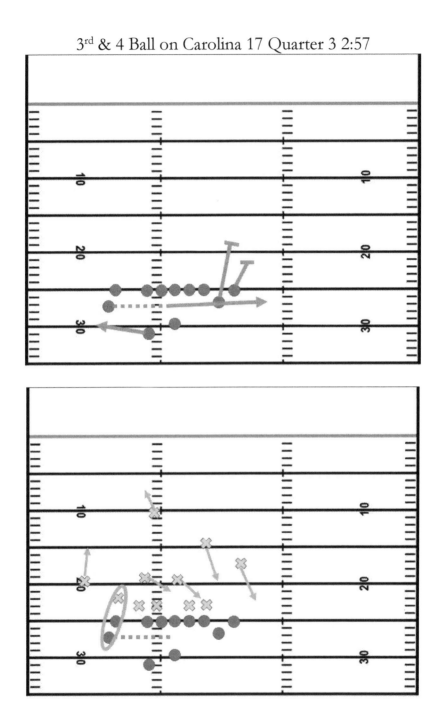

The Saints call a jet sweep on this particular third down. The offensive line blocks inside zone to the left, away from the jet sweep. They also leave the 5 technique to the defense's left unblocked.

The play gets to the edge quickly as the runner gets around the unblocked defender, who hesitates for a second after the ball is snapped. This gives the runner a chance to pick up the first down.

The right tackle is a step slow, and is unable to get in front of the inside linebacker, who helps make the tackle right at the first down marker. The defender who runs across the formation with the motion is the first defender to make the tackle

After review, the play is called back, bringing up a forth and one.

3rd & 13   Ball on Carolina 16   3rd Quarter 0:38

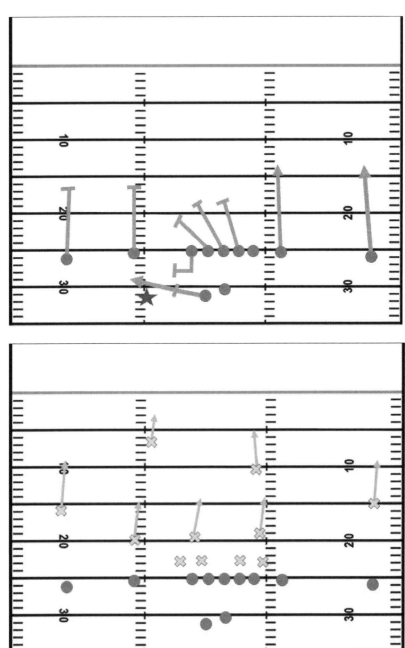

The Saints call a delayed swing screen to their running back, a safe call on third and long when you are in field goal range. The low risk ensures the Saints will still have a shot at a field goal if they do not convert.

Both guards and center release to block the middle linebacker and safeties. The Saints get a nice block from the slot on the left, but not from the outside receiver.

The corner back recognizes the play and triggers the screen route. He makes the tackle with the help of the middle linebacker, to bring up a fourth down.

3rd & 7 Ball on own 42 Quarter 4 10:12

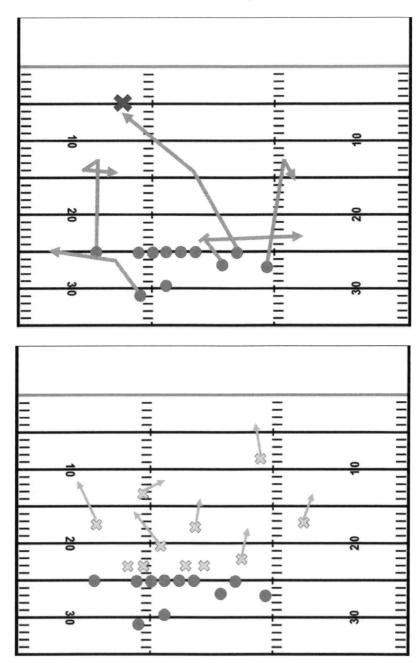

Coverage Read (vs single high safety):

Three on two horizontal/vertical stress on the flat & hook defenders to the offense's left.

The Saints use a creative constraint to one of their basic concepts to try and get a big play on this third down. The Hank concept is a whole-field curl flat concept they will often use a few times each game. Once the defenders recognize these patters, they jump the curl route. The corner bites down, leaving a nice void deep down the left sideline.

Brees makes the throw to the open seam route, but the ball sails up the field and falls incomplete. A missed opportunity when the Saints needed it most.

3rd & 2   Ball on own 37   4th Quarter 6:08

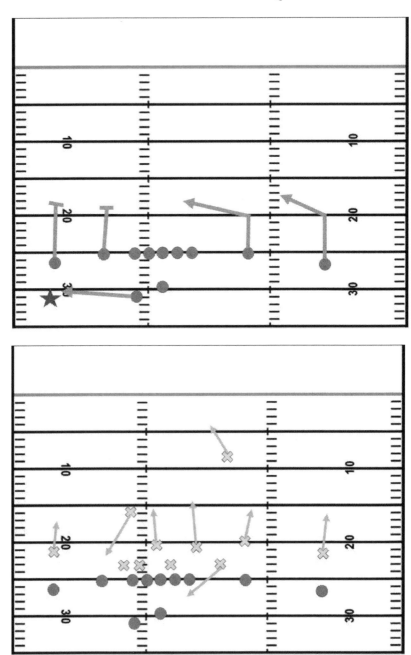

Progression Read:

1. Inside Slant
2. Outside Slant
3. Swing Screen

The Saints use another quick game concept on third and short. The Panthers wise up, and play a more aggressive cover three. Once the screen is recognized by the flat defender on the defense's right, he triggers hard to the outside, which will force the running back to cut it inside to an inside linebacker.

With enough space for the outside slant route, Brees elects to hit the swing route instead. The blocks are good enough, and the running back is able to drag the defender and extra yard to pick up the first down.

3rd & Goal   Ball on Carolina 8   4th Quarter 2:56

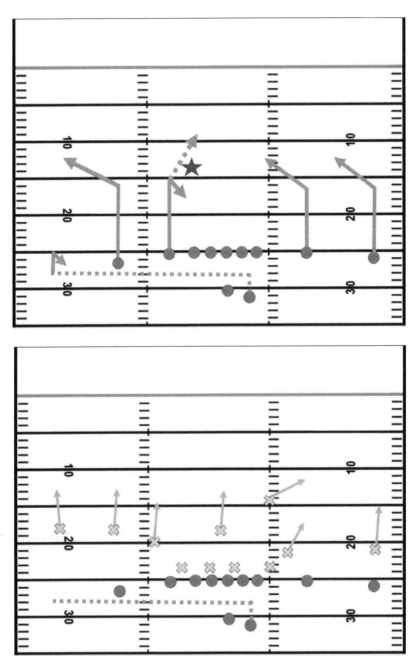

Progression Read:

1. Corner Route
2. Option route (#3 on right)
3. Inside Post
4. Outside Post

The Saints are trying to isolate the tight end on an option route on third and goal. The other routes are meant to take advantage of the defense if they bracket the #3 receiver running the option route.

The Panthers drop their middle linebacker deep, taking away the split route in the option tree. This leaves a nice void for the tight end to sit down in just past the goal line. Brees hits the tight end on the hitch route, and the Saints score a touchdown.

Week 12 vs Los Angeles

3rd & 14   Ball on own 49   1st Quarter 9:23

Progression Read:

1. Curl on the left
2. #2 Dig
3. #1 Dig
4. RB Check Down

The Saints call a Y-Cross variation on their first third down of the game. The single receiver runs a curl at the sticks while the 2 receivers to the right run deep ins. Against a single high safety coverage, the deep curl route should have a 1 on 1. IF an underneath defender brackets the curl, the windows for the digs will be much wider.

The defense plays man coverage with the FS robbing the middle of the field, while everyone else blitzes. The FS takes away the inside dig leaving a window for the outside dig. The receiver does a great job of stemming and getting inside his man, but ends up slipping out of his break causing an incompletion.

3rd & 7   Ball on LA 36   1st Quarter 4:55

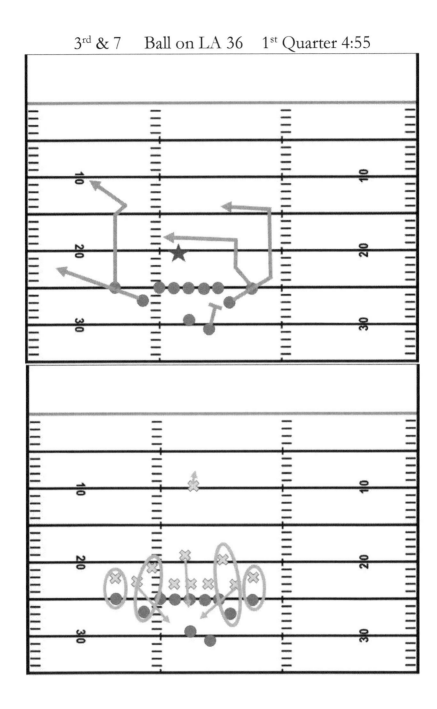

Progression Read:
1. Corner
2. Flat
3. Shallow
4. Dig

Facing a 3rd and 7, the Saints compress their formation with a WR and TE to the left and 2 WR to the right. They run a Smash variation to the left side with the WR running a corner route and the TE running the flat. They bring a variation of the drive concept in from the back side.

With the defense playing man coverage, both frontside routes are covered. Brees then resets his feet to his 3rd read, the shallow. The WR is able to get good separation from his defender and Brees is able to fire it in for a 1st down.

3rd & Goal   Ball on LA 3   1st Quarter 3:06

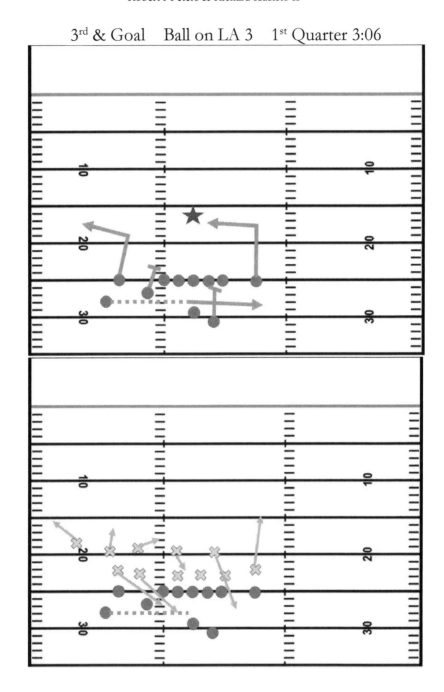

While being near the goal line is a great sign your offense is moving the ball, it also presents some extra challenges for the offense. The closer to the goal line you are, the less space you have to operate as the field shrinks vertically.

The Saints use motion to try and get defenders to move and get themselves out of position. The motion on this play does just that. Brees snaps the ball when the WR is just about to the Center and the 2 LB's to the right come flying down field. This leaves a void behind them for the dig route and Brees finds his WR wide open in the end zone for the touchdown.

3rd & 1   Ball on LA 10   2nd Quarter 10:22

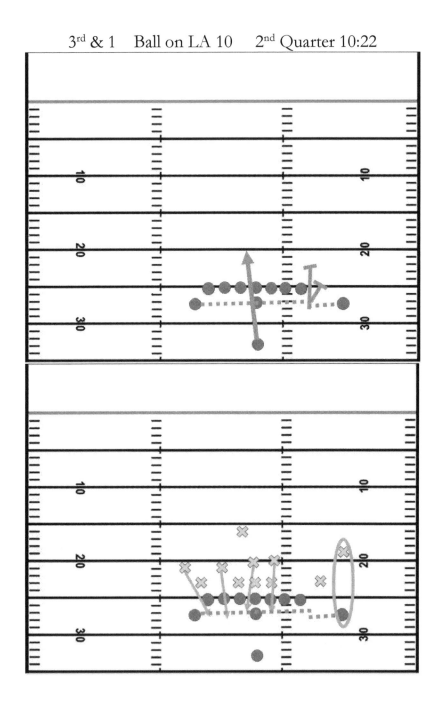

With 3rd and 1 in front of them, the Saints decided to play big boy football and just try and out muscle the defense. The Saints send the wing on the left into motion to the right and then short motion in the WR in also to gain as many blockers as possible.

The defense, knowing it will most likely be run also, flies downhill to the RB as he tries to pick up the 1st down of the left guard. Multiple defenders contribute on the tackle and hold the Saints on 3rd and short.

3rd & Goal   Ball on LA 1   2nd Quarter 8:10

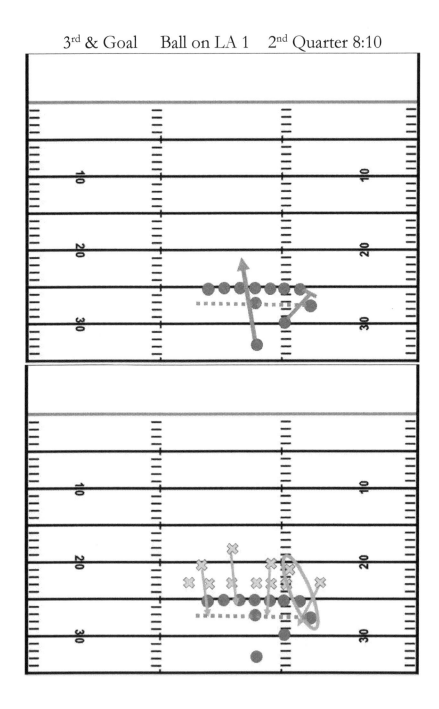

Much like the previous 3rd and short, the Saints bring in the big men (23 personnel meaning 2 running back and 3 TE). Again, the offense motions the wing across the formation to try and gain a numbers advantage. Once again the RB hits the hole off the left guard and again the defense is able to stuff the run and bring up a 4th down.

3rd & 1   Ball on 50   2nd Quarter 4:08

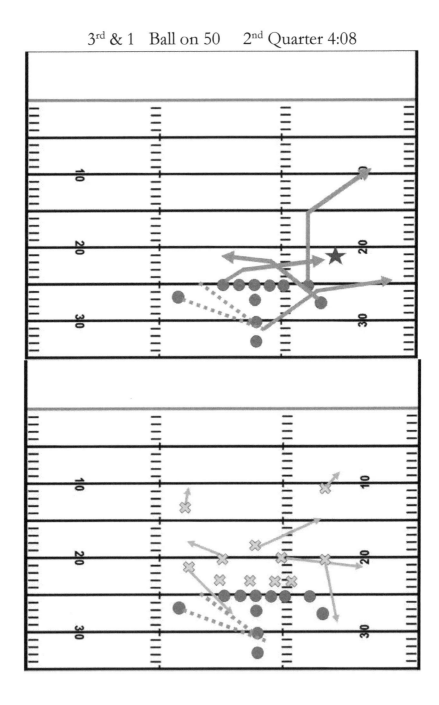

Progression Read:

1. Corner Route
2. Flat route
3. Drag Route (left to right)
4. Drag Route (right to left)

While the final product on this 3rd down was just the basic mesh play, the way in which the Saints got there was creative. The Saints line up a TE in the FB position then motion him out to the left just outside the tackle. Brees then sends the WR to that side in motion and the WR lines up in the spot the FB would right behind Brees.

With a 3rd and short it is safe to assume that the defense will play man coverage and bring pressure to try and stop any run attempt. That is why the Saints moved their personnel around because a LB would be assigned to the WR and a CB would get the TE if the defense did play man. Unfortunately for the offense, the defense plays zone and actually has this play covered well. Brees is able to squeak a pass into is TE through tight window for the 1st down.

3ʳᵈ & 17   Ball on LA 21   3ʳᵈ Quarter 13:05

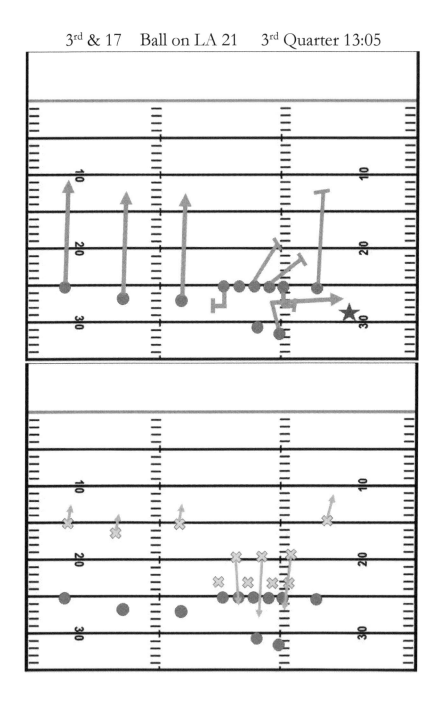

If you were to google "perfectly timed screen pass", this would surely be at the top of that list. After having 2 straight negative plays on 1st and 2nd down, the Saints find themselves in a 3rd and very long. The defense knowing they have a long way to the 1st down marker, plays off man coverage and blitzes everybody else. Just as the LB's are about to get to Brees, he flicks the ball out to his RB who has nothing but green grass in front of him as he coast into the end zone for touchdown.

3rd & 2   Ball on LA 43   3rd Quarter 10:38

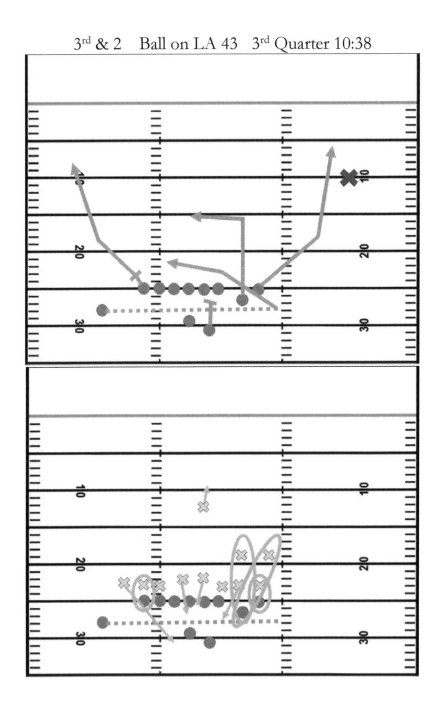

Progression Read:

1. Alert: Fade on right
2. Fade on left
3. Drag
4. Dig

With another 3rd and short in this game, the Saints line up with 2 WR to the right and a TE and WR to the left. Brees then motions over the WR from left to right as he ends with a bunch formation to the right.

The CB follows the WR all the way across indicating man coverage. Knowing this, Brees eyes the fade route on the right the whole way but the pass falls incomplete.

3rd & 8   Ball on own 10   3rd Quarter 6:10

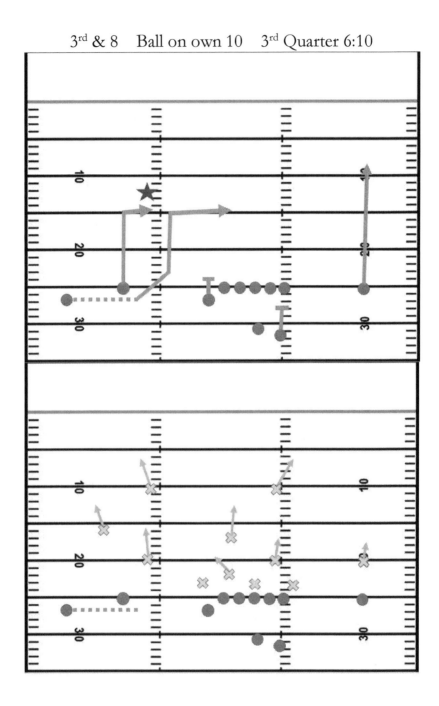

For this 3rd down, the Saints decide to keep their TE and RB in to block to help keep the pressure off of Brees. The defense however only rushes 3 and drops the remain 8 into coverage. The 2 deep safeties drop so deep that they aren't even a factor in this play.

With the double dig backside, the offense is reading the reaction of the LB and whoever he covers the offense will throw opposite. The LB follows the inside dig, leaving a window for Brees to get the ball to his outside dig for the 1st down.

3rd & 4   Ball on own 49   4th Quarter 10:26

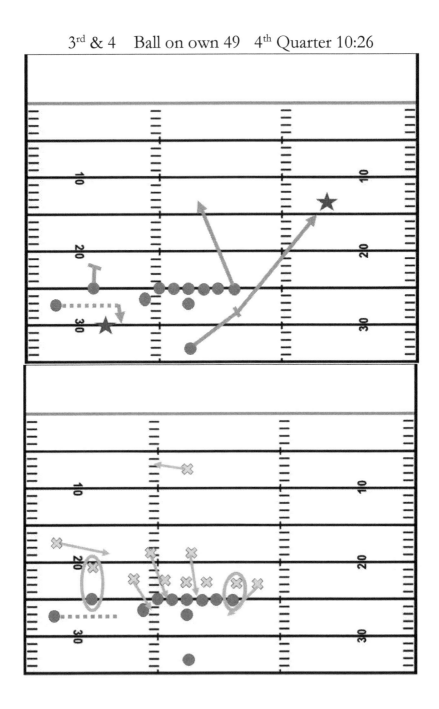

No, you didn't bump your head, there are multiple stars on this play as the offense reaches into its bag of tricks for this 3rd down.

Brees short motions in the WR to the left and throws the ball out to him looking like a quick screen. Meanwhile, the RB is streaking down the right side of the field wide open. The Saints caught the Rams in a blitz and with the TE seam holding the safety, no one gets over to the running back. The WR sets his feet and launches the ball out to the RB for the 1st down and a touchdown.

3rd & 6 Ball on own 37 Quarter 4 7:33

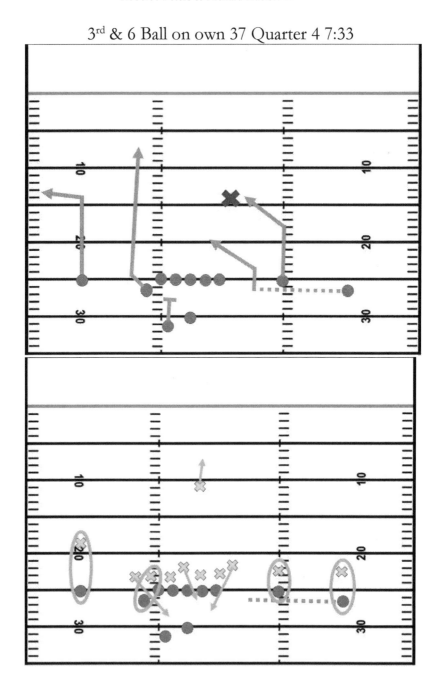

After giving up a few big plays playing soft coverage, the defense goes back to playing man coverage and bringing the heat. The Saints have a verticals concept on the left with double slants to the right. Brees shorts motions in the WR on the outside to the right to get a rub and help the WR get separation from his man.

This technique works and the outside WR has a nice cushion from his defender for an easy catch. Unfortunately for Brees, the pass rush is able to tip the ball at the line of scrimmage and the pass falls to the turf incomplete.

Week 13 vs Detroit

3ʳᵈ & 1   Ball on own 27   1ˢᵗ Quarter 13:36

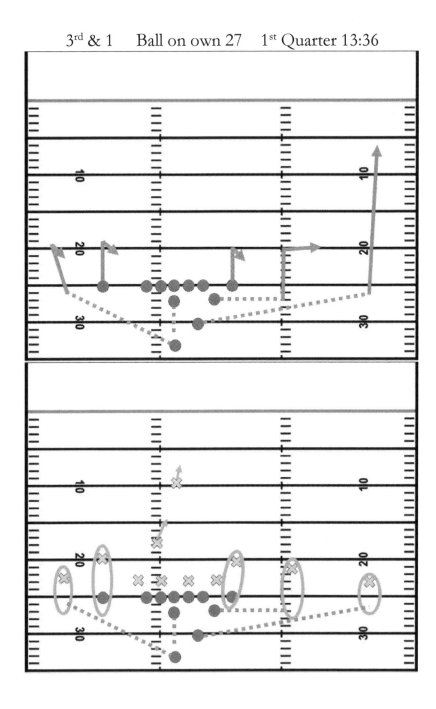

Coverage Read:

1. Pick a side based on matchups and leverage
2. Read outside – in

The Saints shift out of a tight formation, and split out all of the tight ends and running backs out wide. The goal of the shift is to see what the coverage is, and to allow the quarterback to take advantage of any confusion with the quick game pass concept.

The hitches and stick combinations are effective ways to get the ball out of the quarterback's hands quickly, negating any pressure that the defense might bring.

The ball is snapped over the QB's head, which forces the Saints to punt on fourth down.

3rd & 1   Ball on own 47   1st Quarter 6:49

The Saints are faced with a second consecutive third and one. This time, they play it more conservatively. They call a lead run out of the I-formation.

The Lions don't shift much with the motion, suggesting zone coverage. The tight end and left tackle do a nice job of blocking their defenders out. The center and left guard do a nice job of double teaming the 1 technique and climbing to the middle linebacker. The fullback leads up on the outside linebacker.

The three technique on the opposite side of the line gets nice penetration, and tackles the tailback for no gain, bringing up fourth down.

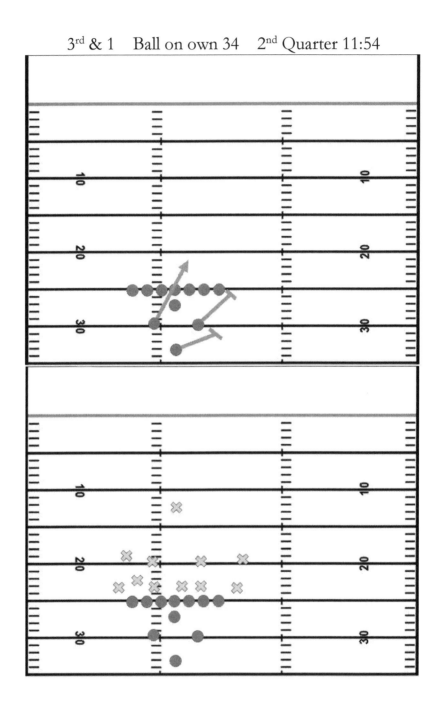

3rd & 1   Ball on own 34   2nd Quarter 11:54

With a third consecutive third and one to start the game, the Saints call a quick dive play out of the inverted wish-bone.

The Center and left guard double team the one technique on the left, and the right guard and right tackle take care of the down lineman on the right.

The unblocked middle linebacker hesitates for a second because of the tricky backfield action, which gives the Saints enough time to pick up the first down.

3ʳᵈ & 10   Ball on own 37   2ⁿᵈ Quarter 11:10

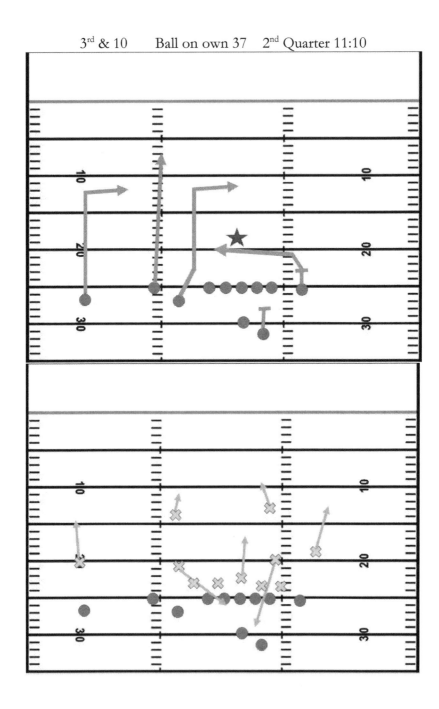

Progression Read:

1. Inside Dig
2. Seam
3. Drag
4. Outside Dig

The Saints call a four vertical constraint on third and long. The play is a shallow cross concept that is designed to look like four verticals initially. The play gives a the quarterback an easy progression to try and find an open receiver.

The Lions bring some pressure, which forces Brees to escape the pocket to his right. This is very convenient for the Lions defense, because the read on the play is to his left.

Brees throws across his body to the drag route, which gets tackled for a short gain. This brings up a fourth down.

3ʳᵈ & 13   Ball on Detroit 24   2ⁿᵈ Quarter 5:49

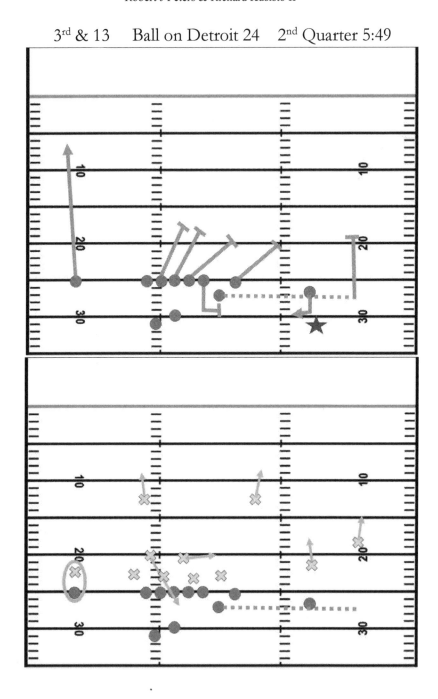

Playing it safe on third and long, the Saints call a quick screen to the middle man in the trips formation. The interior of the line breaks laterally to block the screen, while the right tackle pass sets to block the rushing defensive end.

The Lions come out in a two high safety shell, trying to keep any completions in front of them.

The Lions' defensive line does a nice job of pursuing to the screen, and make the tackle after a short gain of three. This brings up a fourth down for the Saints.

3rd & 6   Ball on own 30   2nd Quarter 0:29

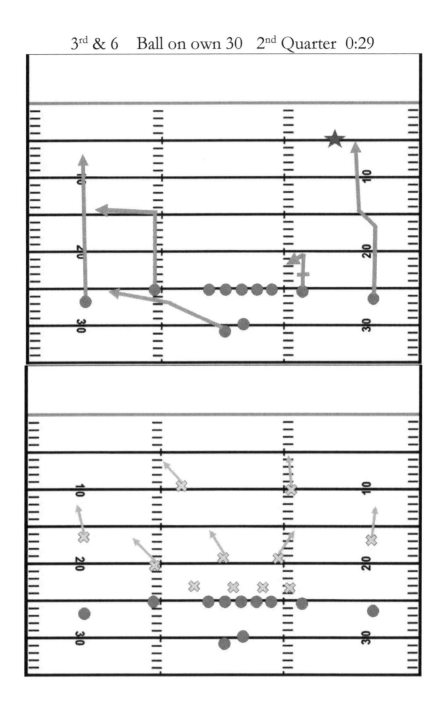

With time running out in the half, the Saints call a slick double move concept. The play is meant to look like the dig-hitch back side combination that they typically use. The Saints want the safety to identify this, so he will trigger up. The safety takes the bait, and the double move works. The corner hesitates, and it placed in a trail technique on the steaking split end.

With time winding down, the double move is a last chance effort to get a big play before the half.

This play gets the Saints into field goal range, and allows them to pick up a field goal just before half time.

3rd & 6   Ball on own 29 3rd   Quarter 7:51

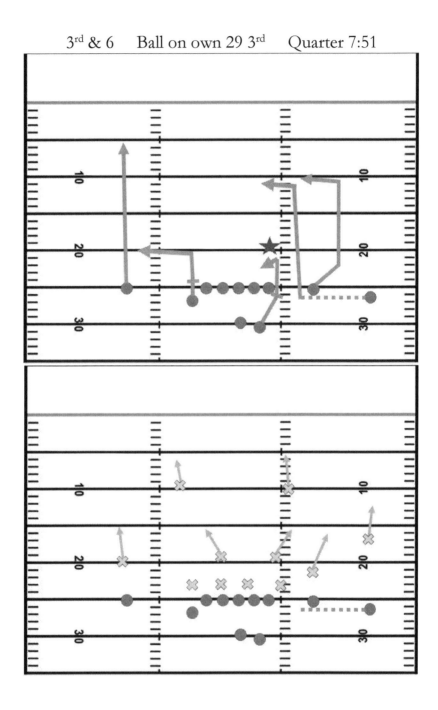

Progression Read:

1. Fade
2. Speed out (chip release)
3. Inside Dig
4. Outside Dig
5. RB Check down (chip release)

The Saints call a Y cross variation on this third down. The two chip-releases by the underneath route runners to give the play more time to develop. This all-purpose play works against any coverage. The six yards needed does not preclude the quarterback from taking a check down, either.

The Lions play a split safety coverage, with the underneath defenders getting quite a bit of depth, considering the distance needed.

Brees cycles through his progression, and gets to his last read on the play. He dumps the ball off to the running back, and picks up the first down.

3rd & 12   Ball on own 35   3rd Quarter 6:30

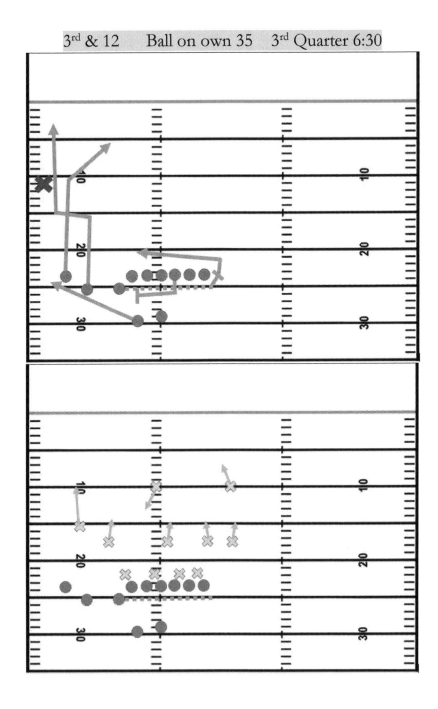

Progression Read:

1. Out n' Up (Double Move)
2. Flat route from RB
3. TE chip release drag

The Saints get creative on this third and long. They run a double move at the first down marker. This situation is one of the best times to run a double move. The defense is expecting a route to break at the sticks, so they will be more likely to jump the shorter route.

There seems to be a mix up for the Saints. The guard pulls to simulate run action, yet there is no backfield fake.

The Lions roll their coverage to the short side of the field, in prime position to cover the concept. The safety buzzes down to become the hook defender. He stays deep, knowing the down and distance. This allows him to undercut the double move, and intercept the pass.

3rd & 6   Ball on Detroit 10   4th Quarter 14:18

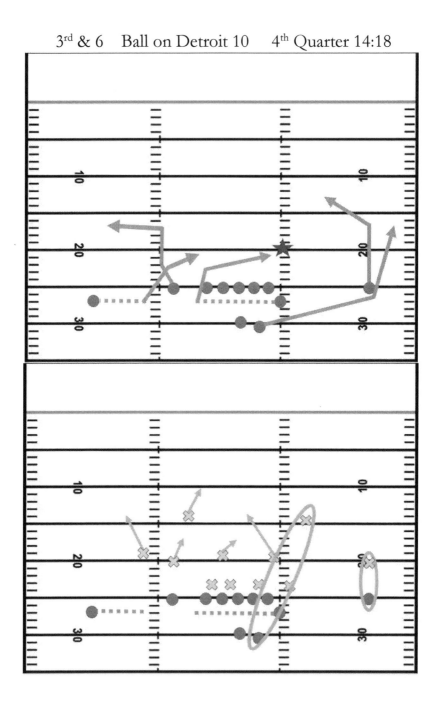

Progression Read

1. Post
2. Wheel/Swing
3. TE Drag
4. WR Drag

The Saints shift the tight end, before motioning the outside receiver to create a stack on the left.

With the Lions playing man on the short side of the field, Brees looks to hit the tight end or split end on the underneath drag routes. He passes these routes up and buys some more time by moving around the pocket.

He ends up hitting the split end on the drag route on the right side of the field, and the Saints pick up a first down.

3rd & 10   Ball on own 35   4th Quarter 10:26

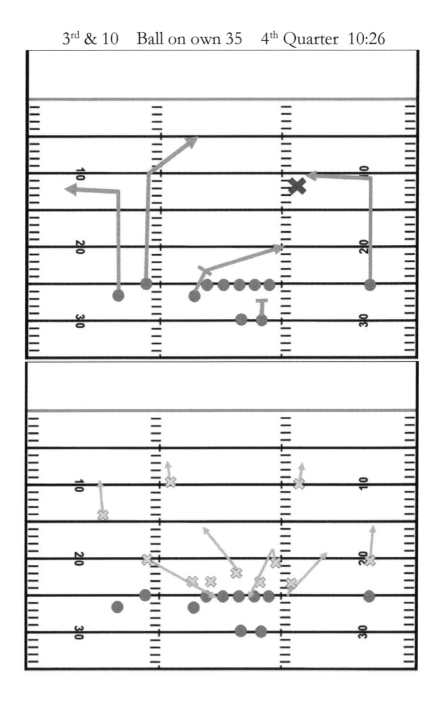

The Saints call a version of the shallow cross series out of trips. They bring the dig from the short side of the field, and protect it with a post from the slot on the right. Many teams read the shallow cross series differently, so it is hard to determine how the play reads for the Saints.

The Lions bail out of a blitz look, only to bring other defenders on a blitz instead. This play is worth a look on Game Pass if you enjoy creative defensive pressures.

The Saints' offensive line is unable to pick up all 5 rushers, even with the running back staying in to protect. Brees is forced to throw the dig early, and the corner makes a tremendous break on the route to break up the pass attempt.

3rd & 14   Ball on own 21   4th Quarter 6:17

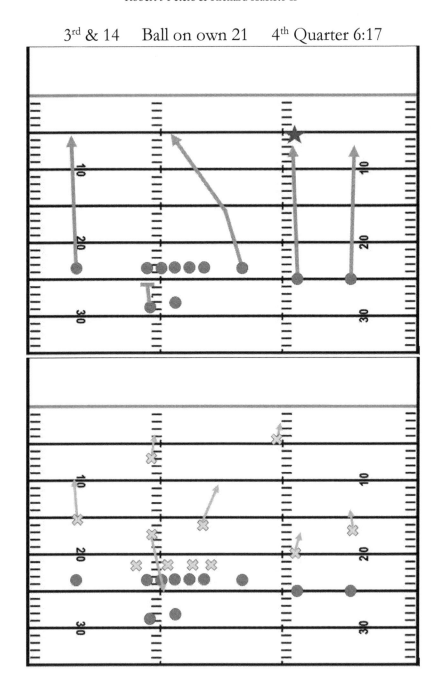

Coverage Read

1. Vs single high safety: throw the slot seam away from the rotation.
2. Vs two high safeties: pick a side and throw one of the verticals away from that safety.

On this third and forever, the Saints call four verticals. The Lions are in a two shell, but the weak safety rolls post snap to rob any inside routes from the trips side of the field.

Brees notices the right safety cheating inside, and he fires the ball to the seam by the #2 receiver. This is great technique from the receiver, exactly how you want to run a seam route if the man on you is playing with outside leverage. Great teaching tape.

3ʳᵈ & 10   Ball on own 45   4ᵗʰ Quarter 1:08

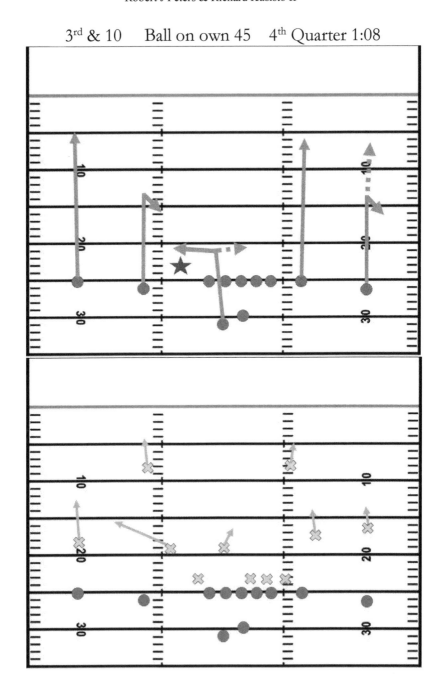

Coverage Read

1. Vs single high safety: throw the slot seam away from the rotation.
2. Vs two high safeties: pick a side and throw one of the verticals away from that safety.

With the game out of reach, the Saints call four verticals again. The Lions play a prevent.

Brees hits the back out of the backfield to keep the chains moving.

3rd & 4 Ball on Detroit 14 Quarter 4 :02

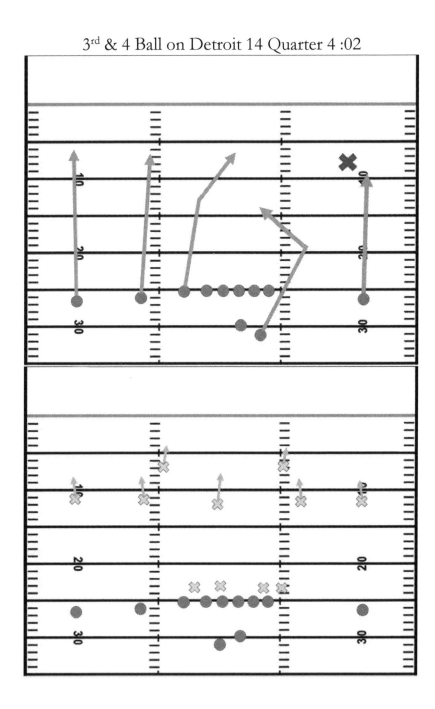

Coverage Read

3. Vs single high safety: throw the slot seam away from the rotation.
4. Vs two high safeties: pick a side and throw one of the verticals away from that safety.

With the game out of reach, the Saints call four verticals again. The Lions play prevent.

The ball is thrown up for grabs in the end zone. The Lions intercept the ball to end the game.

Week 14 at Tampa Bay

3rd & 6   Ball on own 24   1st Quarter 11:51

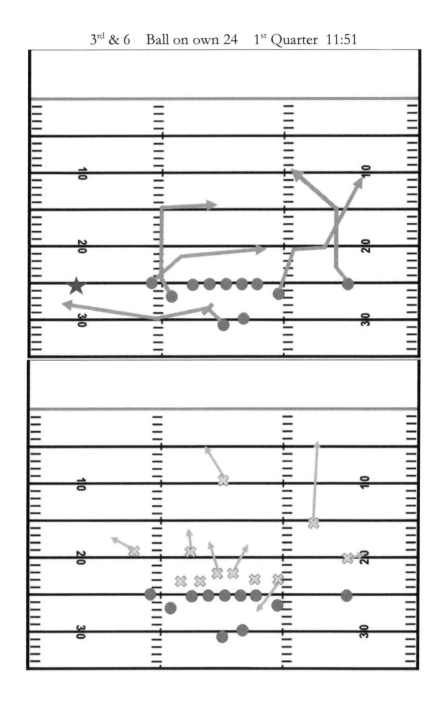

Progression Read:

1. Peak Post
2. Wheel
3. Drag
4. Dig
5. RB Check Down

The Saints call one of their go-to third down calls on this third and medium. They call a frontside concepts with their backside two man drive combination.

The Buccaneers show blitz, then back out into a cover two. They sit on the sticks, not allowing the Saints to get an easy completion at the first down marker.

Brees cycles through his progression, and has enough time to get to his last read. The running back gets tackled by the corner and the Saints are forced to punt.

3ʳᵈ & 5   Ball on own 22   1ˢᵗ Quarter 6:46

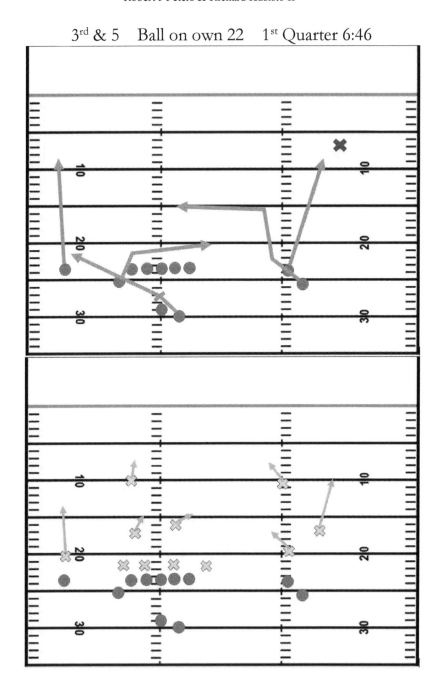

Coverage Read:

1. If no safety help on outside, throw the fade route
2. If safety help or off coverage, read deep cross to check down

The Saints call this Y cross variation on third and medium. This play call is optimized at a medium distance, as the check downs are viable options to still pick up a first down.

The Buccaneers play a quarters match coverage to the wide side of the field. the safety jumps the deep crossing route, giving Brees a chance to hit the fade from the slot.

Brees throws the fade, and the ball falls incomplete with an offensive pass interference call.

3rd & 8   Ball on own 27   2nd Quarter 7:50

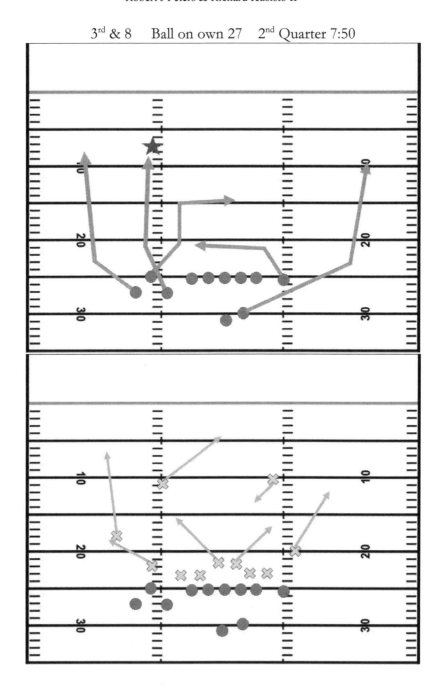

Coverage Read:

1. Vs single high safety: throw opposite the rotation
2. Vs two high safeties: Read Wheel – Dig – Drag

The Saints call a four vertical variation. The play has built in man and two high safety adjustments.

The Buccaneers call cover three, just the coverage the Saints were hoping for. The bunch gives the seam routes a free release. The flat defender leaves the seam route to get more width, leaving the seam route open.

The Saints convert and pick up the first down.

3rd & 10   Ball on Tampa Bay 29   2nd Quarter 6:15

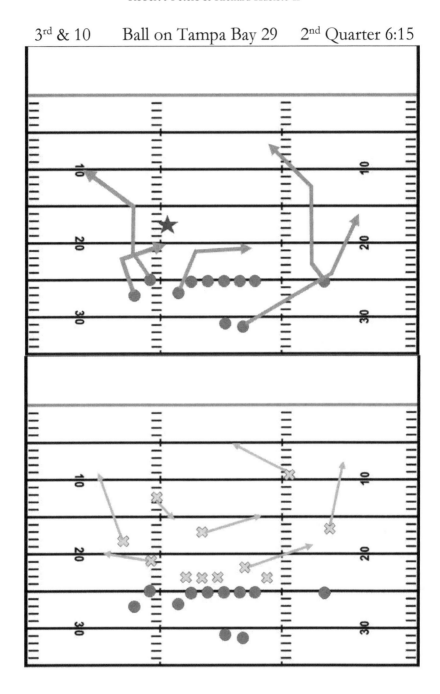

Progression Read

1. Alert: Post
2. RB Wheel
3. Drag
4. Drive

With the Buccaneers playing cover three on this third down, the Saints have another good play call to attack the holes in this zone. The only problem, they need ten yards.

The Buccaneers drop their underneath defenders to the depth of the first down marker. This forces Brees to take the drive route as a check down. The inside linebacker triggers up after the ball is thrown and makes a nice tackle. This keeps the Saints short of the first down and brings up a fourth down.

3rd & 3   Ball on Tampa Bay 32   2nd Quarter 2 3:41

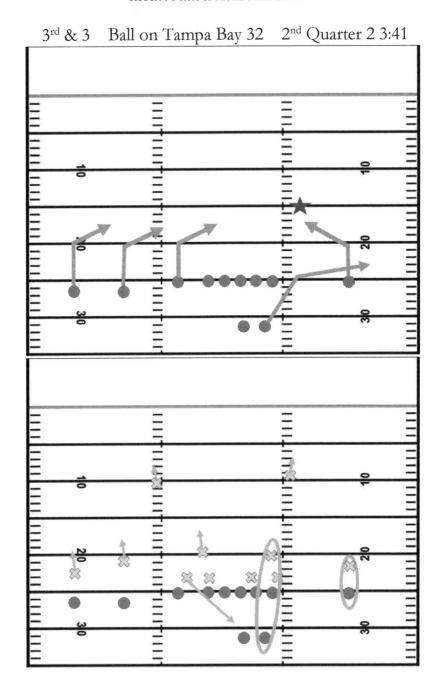

The Saints call a quick game concept to each side of the field on this third down. The QB must decide where he is going with the ball after he sees the initial movement of the middle linebacker.

The Buccaneers call a combination coverage, and play man to the single receiver side. With two high safeties, the corner allows the inside release on the slant.

Brees throws the ball on rhythm, and the Saints pick up the first down.

3rd & 1   Ball on Tampa Bay 14   2nd Quarter 2:24

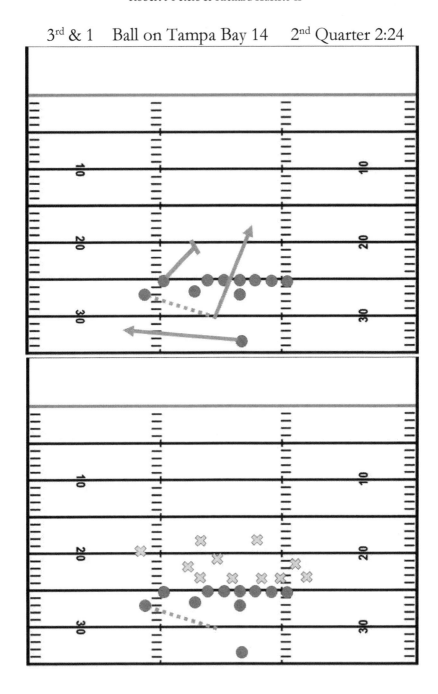

The Saints try and sneak the fullback through with a quick hitting dive play on this third and one. The Saints like to call toss plays with this formation and action. This tendency will cause the linebackers to hesitate, preventing them from helping the defensive line of the play.

The left side of the offensive line gets a good push on the defensive front, which gives the Saints enough wiggle room to pick up a first down

3ʳᵈ & 13   Ball on own 42   3ʳᵈ Quarter 12:28

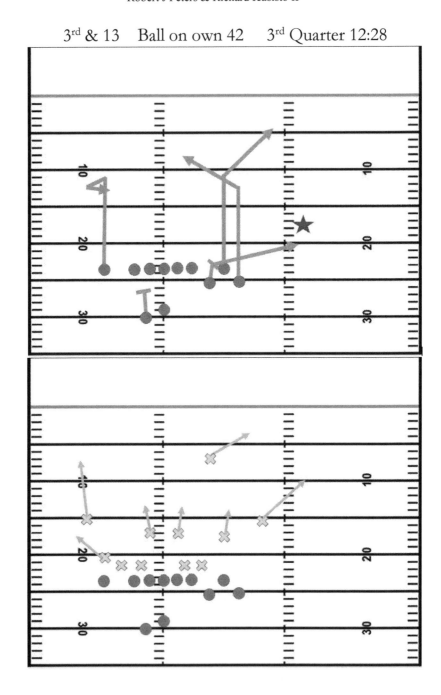

Progression Read:

1. Alert: Post
2. Corner
3. Flat Route
4. 10 Yard Turn Route

The Saints are trying to get an easy shot down the field with the scissors concept on this third and long. They are hoping the corner and safety are occupied with the post route, and slip the corner route behind them.

The Buccaneers roll out of the single high look, and get into a cover two. The corner trails the scissors action, and is in good position to defend the tight end on the corner route. A little pressure gets past the left guard, and forces Brees to escape to his right. Brees takes the check down in the flat, and forces the Saints to punt on fourth down.

3rd & 3   Ball on own 27   3rd Quarter 7:52

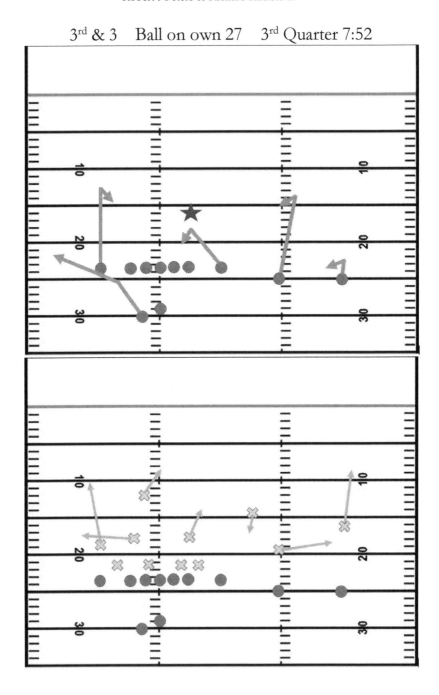

Coverage Read:

1. Throw off the movement of the inside linebacker(s)
2. Spot
3. Curl
4. Flat

The Saints use an inverted curl flat concept to the wide side of the field. This concept works well to the wide side of the field, and it sells vertical releases. The vertical release help prevent defenses from pattern reading the concept. A quick flat from the #2 receiver allows teams to bracket the curl route.

The Buccaneers roll to a cover three, and leave the spot route wide open. They are too worried about disguising the coverage that they are late to rotate.

The Saints get the completion and the first down.

3rd & 2   Ball on Tampa Bay 4   3rd Quarter 3:45

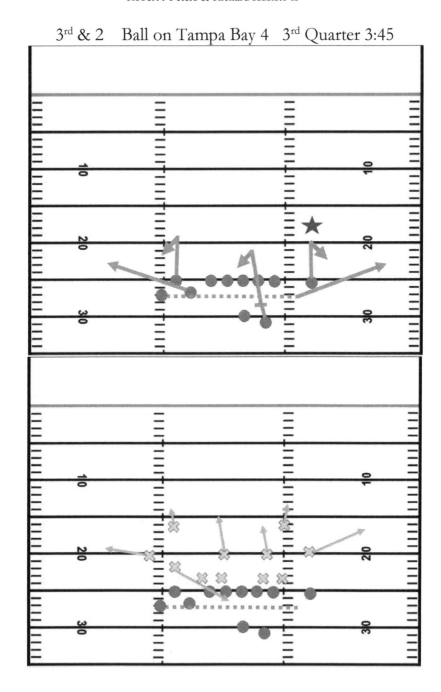

The Saints call the stick concept in the red zone. In a short yardage situation, the stick concept gives the offense versatility. The bunch formation ensures free releases. The play attacks all underneath zones, while creating natural rubs against man coverage.

The outside linebacker gets caught in no-mans-land, between rushing and dropping into his zone. The safety is late to trigger on the stick route to the right, giving the QB an opportunity to fit the ball in.

The Saints get a completion and a touchdown.

3rd & 1   Ball on own 34   4th Quarter 12:22

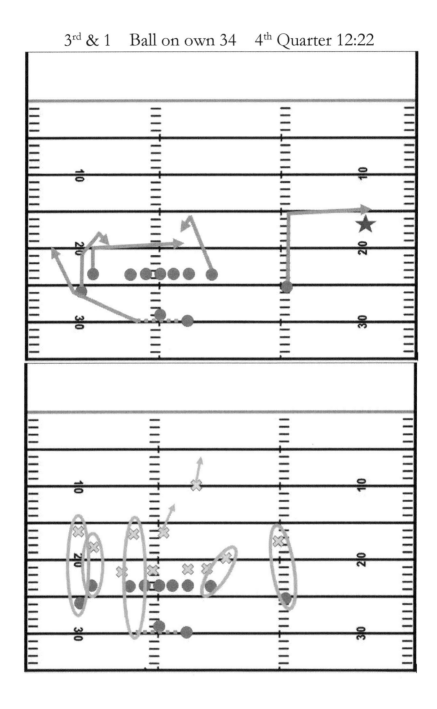

Progression Read:

1. 10 Yard Out
2. Drag
3. TE Spot Route (on right)

    The Saints call a variation of a shallow crossing/mesh concept on this third and one. The spot routes create a natural rub for the drag and the wheel, without the traditional meshing action. This variation gives the offense blitz beaters, while attacking the same zones.

    The one on one coverage is identified, and Brees also notices the inside leverage that the corner is playing with. He throws the deep out cut on rhythm and picks up the first down.

3rd & 1   Ball on Tampa Bay 47   4th Quarter 10:15

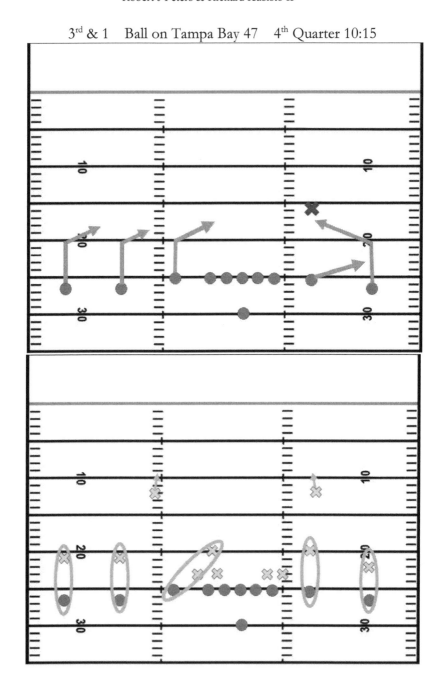

The Saints call a quick game concept on third and one. The double slants concept works well against two high safeties. There are no extra underneath defenders to bracket the inside breaking routes.

The slant – flat combination works well against single high safety coverages. The play attacks the soft edge of these coverages. The movement of the routes allows for more yards after the catch than similar concepts.

Brees decides to hit the slant route to the boundary. The safety on that side of the filed triggers after he sees #2 run to the flat. He over runs the play, but still disrupts it enough for the pass to fall incomplete and bring up a fourth down.

3rd & 2   Ball on own 9   4th Quarter 6:00

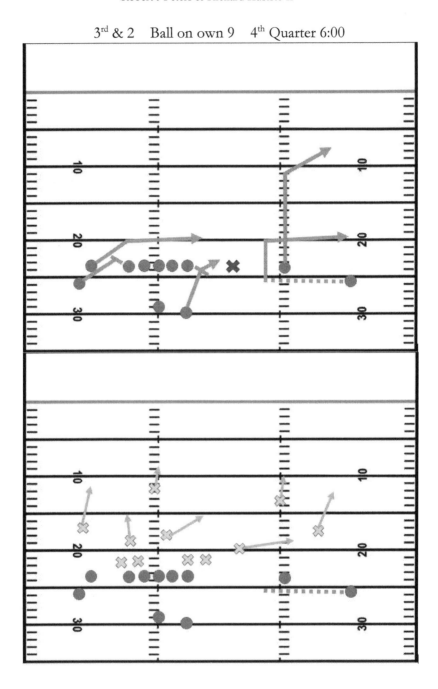

Coverage Read:

Throw off of the movement of the corner back. Hit the quick out or the corner route.

With time in the game winding down, and the Saints behind by five, the pressure to convert third downs amplifies. The Saints call a sprint out smash concept. This half field read is meant to simplify the concept for the quarterback. This will also encourage him to get rid of the ball quicker, as he has only two options to decide to throw to.

With the down and distance being so short, the quick motion is designed to get a free release for the flat route. This throw is supposed to be a safe easy throw for the quarterback.

The Buccaneers match the flat route aggressively. The outside linebacker stays with the flat route, and removes any separation that the short motion created. The corner back plays the corner route well, as he is playing an off coverage. Pressure gets to Brees, and forces an incompletion and fourth down.

3rd & 4   Ball on own 42   4th Quarter 1:08

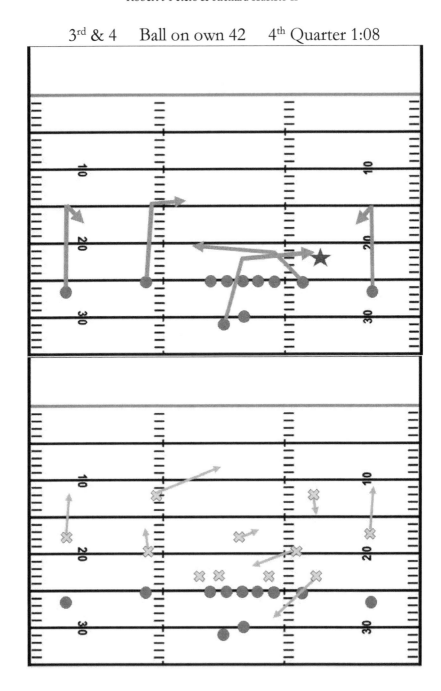

Progression Read: (pre-snap pick a side)

1. Hitch
2. Drag (RB or TE)
3. Dig

The Saints are down to their final drive, still down five points. The Saints call a version of the shallow cross concept. With the outside hitch routes, the Saints have five underneath routes that evenly space out the defense, and create a well-timed play.

Brees sees two high safeties, and assumes the Buccaneers will be in a cover two. This coverage eliminates the hitches on the outside, and he focuses on the inside crossing action. This assumption cost him, as both hitch routes are open on the play.

Brees hits his running back on the check down, and he gets tackled shy of a first down.

Week 15 at Arizona

3rd & 3   Ball on Arizona 30   1st Quarter 8:03

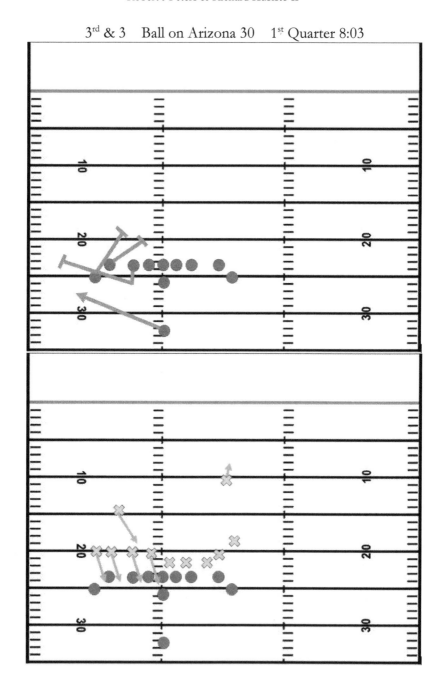

The Saints turn to their go-to toss play on this third and short. The two receivers on the left are charged with getting down blocks on the defensive end and outside linebacker.

The Cardinals edge defenders do a nice job of sniffing the play out. The outside linebacker dodges the block from the outside receiver. The outside receiver gets stuck in no man's land, and abandons the down block to follow the outside linebacker.

The pulling tackle gets confused, and stays outside to stay true to his assignment. The corner cuts inside the tackle's block, but does not make the play.

The Saints pick up about twelve yards and a first down.

3ʳᵈ & 12   Ball on Arizona 21   1ˢᵗ Quarter 6:10

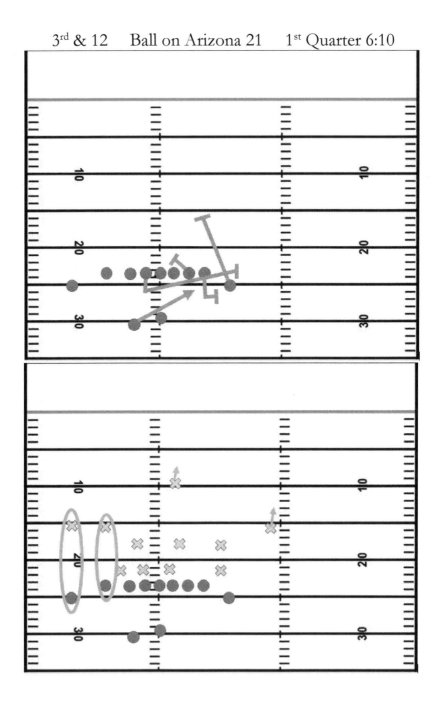

Being in field goal range, the Saints play this third and long conservatively. They call a power scheme, that ends up looking like a trap scheme. The blitzing safety ends up requiring a kick out block by the left guard, as the tight end is blocking the widened defensive end.

The Cardinals play the concept well. With the guard having to kick out the blitzing safety, there is nobody to block the inside linebacker on the play side. He makes the tackle which brings up a fourth down.

3ʳᵈ & 10   Ball on Arizona 10   1ˢᵗ Quarter 1:41

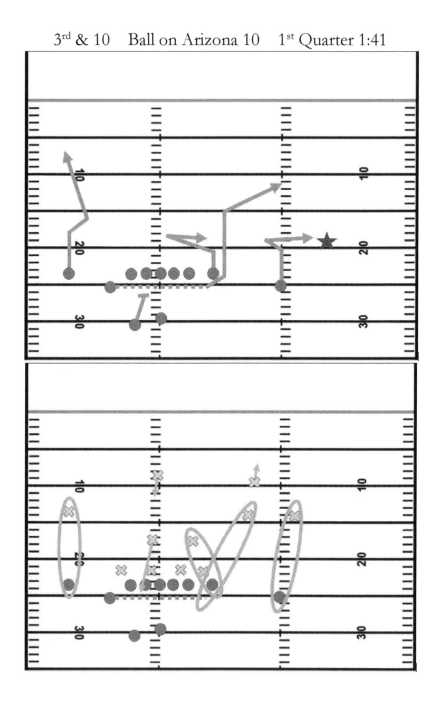

Progression Read:

1. Sluggo (1st receiver on the left)
2. Whip route from #3 on right
3. Corner Route
4. Whip from #1 on right

The Saints call a neat constraint play for their go-to "H Post" or their "Drive" concept. The Sluggo is meant to be the answer against man coverage, or an aggressive zone scheme. If the defense brackets the Sluggo, the whip route should have a one on one with the linebacker.

The Cardinals play off coverage on the Sluggo, covering the route tightly. Brees cycles through his reads quickly to find the whip route on the outside. The Saints get the completion and score a touchdown.

3rd & 2   Ball on Arizona 36   2nd Quarter 9:37

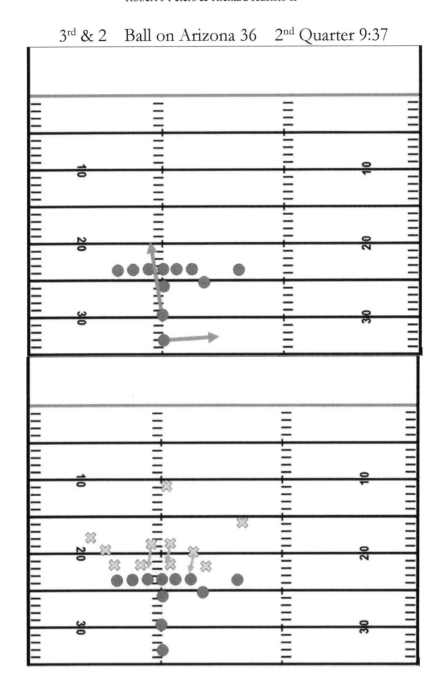

The Saints call the quick hitting fullback dive on third and two. The play is part of a series that includes a flip to the tailback to attack the perimeter.

The Saints get a strong double team on the defensive lineman on the play side. The Cardinals are able to stuff the play with the quick trigger from their inside linebackers to fill the open gaps.

The Cardinals bring the intensity on this play, and force a fourth down.

3rd & 4   Ball on Arizona 45   2nd Quarter 2:00

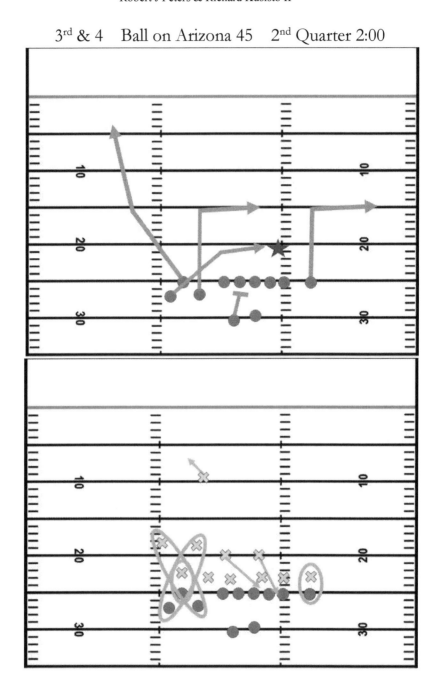

Progression Read:

1. Alert: Fade
2. 10 Yard Out
3. Drag
4. Dig

The Saints call the drive concept out of the bunch formation. The play gives the quarterback a simple progression read that brings his eyes into the flow of each route.

The Cardinals play man coverage, with a banjo technique on the #1 and #3 receiver in the bunch formation.

The straight stem from the dig route forces the inside banjo defender to back pedal, taking him further away from the man he eventually must guard, the drag route.

The receiver running the drag route uses a "stair case" technique on the route. This technique requires the receiver to stem back vertical once he reaches the left tackle. Against man coverage, this technique will create even more separation for the receiver.

Brees hits the drag route, and the receiver turns on the burners and runs for a touchdown.

3rd & 4   Ball on own 28   2nd Quarter 0:08

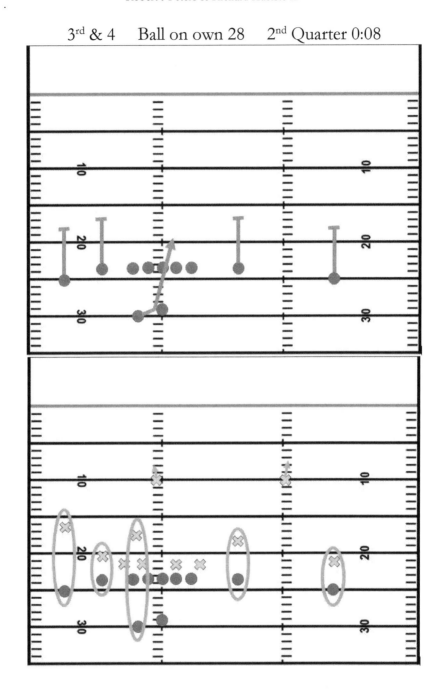

With time winding down in the half, the Saints run a draw play to run out the clock.

The offensive line does a nice job of giving the running back a clear lane to pick up the first down. The center and left guard double team to the middle linebacker.

3rd & 10   Ball on own 25   3rd Quarter 14:49

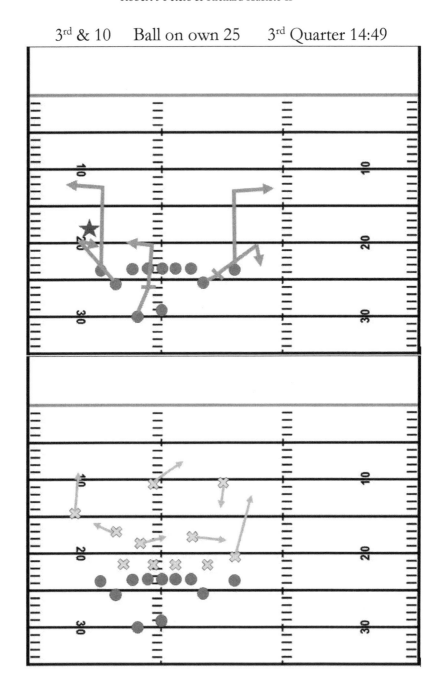

Coverage Read:

Read away from the rotation of the inside linebacker and safety. Read Deep Out – TE Sit – RB Check Down.

With the safety rotating to the offenses right, Brees looks to the two man combination on his left. The corner back is squatting with outside leverage at 10 yards, taking away the deep out cut. Brees is forced to take the tight end on the sit route.

The flat defender comes up and makes the tackle, forcing a fourth down.

3rd & 10   Ball on Arizona 39   3rd Quarter 7:36

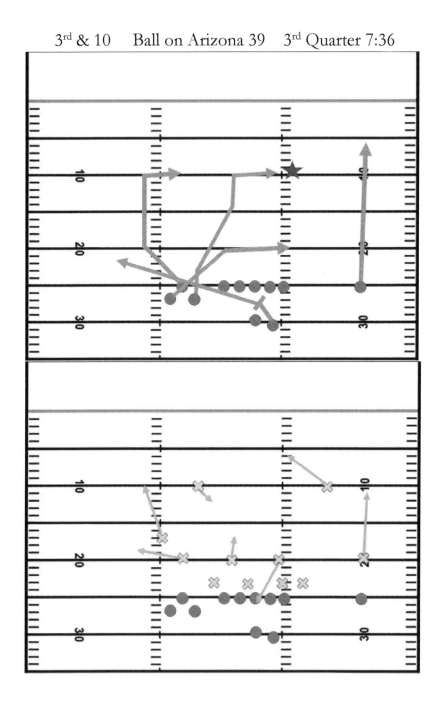

Progression Read:

1. Fade
2. Drag (#1 on the left)
3. Inside Deep Cross (#3 on left)
4. Dig (#2 on the left)
5. RB Check Down

The Saints call a Y cross variation on this third and long, giving the quarterback a few deeper targets.

The Cardinals play a "box" coverage to the bunch formation. The "box" call gives the defense four defenders on the three receivers to the left.

The Y cross variation floods the part of the field that the "box" call is weakest, on the single receiver side. The safety to the short side of the field gets too much depth, and takes himself out of the play. The deep cross from the #3 receiver runs away from the safety to the wide side of the field, giving Brees an easy target to pick up the first down.

3rd & 5   Ball on Arizona 21   3rd Quarter 6:15

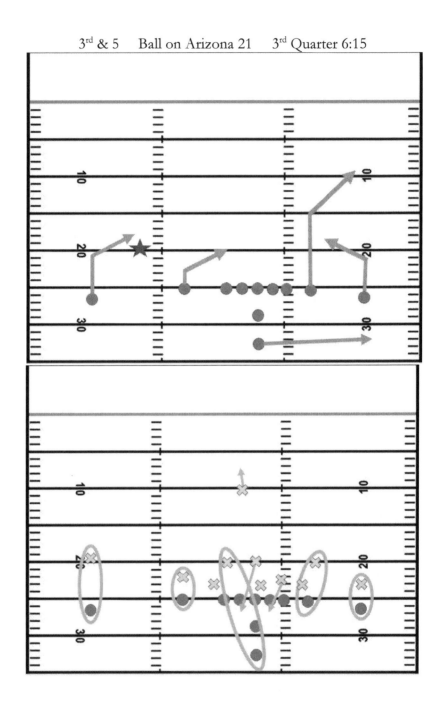

Coverage Read:

1. Vs single high safety: Read Snag concept on the right (flat – spot)
2. Vs two high safeties: read slants on left (inside – out)
3. Vs man: pick matchups and leverage that favor the offense

The Saints give their quarterback a half field read on this third down. The play allows the quarterback to pre-determine which side of the field he will read before the ball is snapped.

With the Cardinals playing man coverage, Brees likes the cushion he sees on the outside receiver to his left. He catches the snap and fires the ball to the outside. The pass falls low and incomplete.

3rd & 1   Ball on Arizona 32   3rd Quarter 0:36

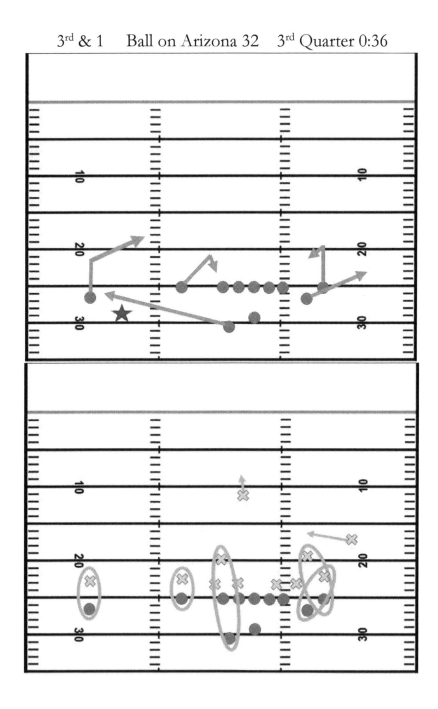

The Saints call a man beater on this third down.

With the offense only needing one yard, the Cardinals play tight man coverage. They play three defenders over the two man bunch to the offenses right in order to take away any quick crossing action.

They did not account for any rubs on the other side of the field. the slot receiver comes down and bumps into the middle linebacker, giving the running back the outside leverage he needs.

The Saints pick up about fifteen yards and a first down.

3rd & 9   Ball on Arizona 14   4th Quarter 13:51

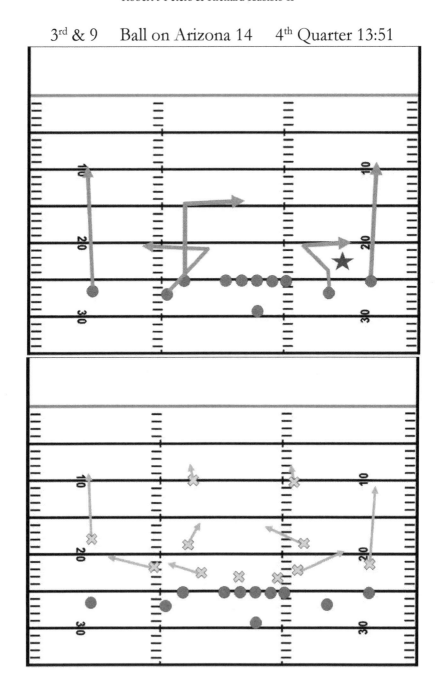

The Saints call a mirrored whip concept, with a dig route coming from the three receiver side. The play puts the middle linebacker in a high – low bind vs a two high safety. Against a single high safety, the whip on the left should have leverage to get to the flat.

The Cardinals call an exotic coverage, and only rush two. They attempt to bracket the inside receivers, playing three over two to the wide side of the field, and playing inside – out on the slot to the right.

The dropping defensive end initially takes himself out of the play, allowing a completion. He makes up for it, and tackles the ball carrier short of a first down.

3rd & 8   Ball on Arizona 27   4th Quarter 4:29

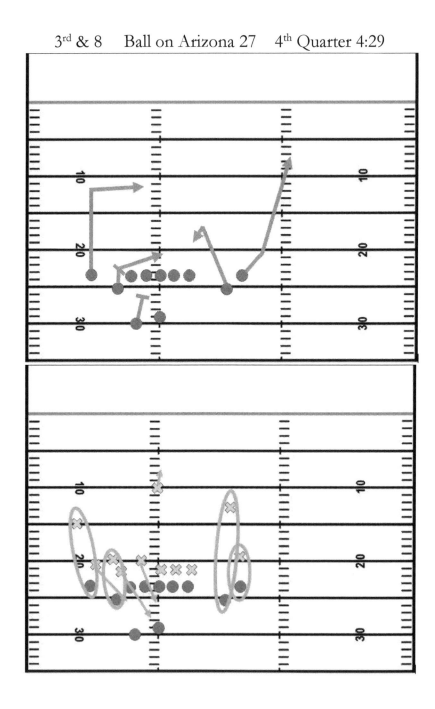

Progression Read:

1. Alert: Fade
2. Spot Route
3. Dig
4. Drag Chip – Release

The Saints call a blitz beater two man frontside combination, with a backside high low to give the quarterback a nice progression. If the defense brings a zone blitz, the spot route will open up in the void. Against man, the fade should be able to get leverage to create a one on one.

The Cardinals turn up the heat and rush six, playing cover 1 behind it. Playing off man coverage against the compressed formations gives the Cardinals the ability to break quickly on any route near the first down marker. Getting quick pressure on the quarterback will not allow him to get the ball down the field to the deeper breaking routes after 10 yards.

Brees feels the free rusher and can't find the open spot route. Brees gets sacked and the Saints are forced to punt.

3rd & 2   Ball on Arizona 5   4th Quarter 3:38

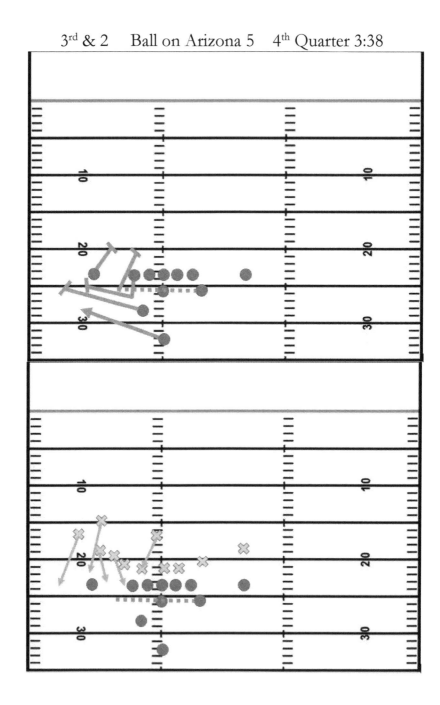

The Saints call their toss concept in another short yardage situation. The motion gives the Saints an extra man at the point of attack in order to get the down block on the defensive end. This time, the Saints have a fullback as an extra puller to block an extra force defender.

The Cardinals get an extra defender to flow to the toss play. the extra defender gets mixed up in all the traffic with the pulling tackle and fullback.

The tailback follows his blockers nicely to pick up a first down.

3rd & 4 Ball on Arizona 46 Quarter 4 2:00

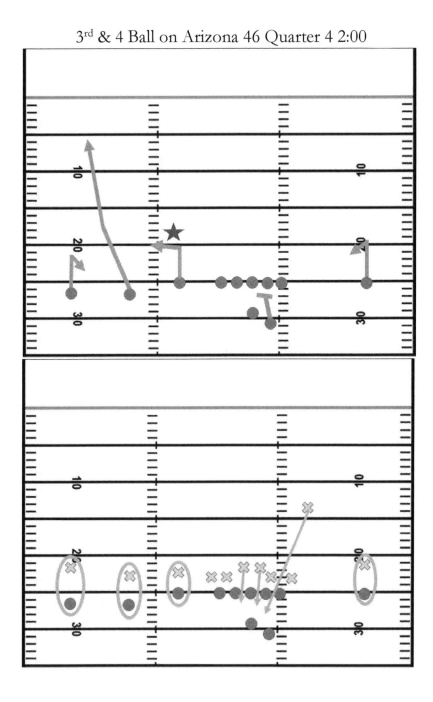

With the Saints clinging to a one possession lead, they call one of their go – quick game concepts to try to put the Cardinals away. The slot fade concept gives the quarterback a few short options, as well as a shot play if the defense plays aggressively.

The Cardinals try to turn the tide of the game by calling a cover zero blitz.

The tight end gets nice separation at the top of his stem on the stick route (maybe with the help of a little push off). The Saints get a completion and their final first down of the game.

.

Week 16 vs Tampa Bay

3rd & 5   Ball on Tampa Bay 46   1st Quarter 12:02

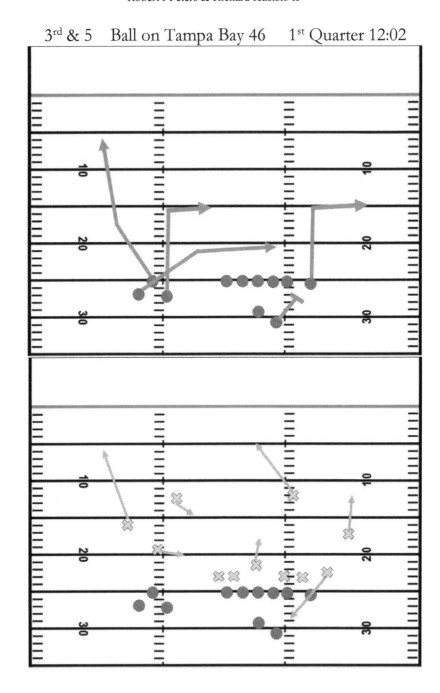

Progression Read:

1. Alert: Fade
2. 10 Yard Out
3. Drag
4. Dig

The Saints call their drive concept out of trips on third and medium. The concept gives the quarterback an option against most coverages. There seems to be a miscommunication with the protection, as the back and center both react to the blitzer.

The Buccaneers rush five and play a fire zone (3 deep, 3 under). The corner to the short side of the field sticks the tight end running the 10 yard out. This man coverage allows the flat defender (dropping linebacker over the nose) to peel inside and help on the drag. The buzzing safety is in perfect position to wall off the dig route.

The perfect coverage from the Buccaneers forces Brees to hang on to the ball too long, and gets sacked.

3rd & 1   Ball on own 28   1st Quarter 4:59

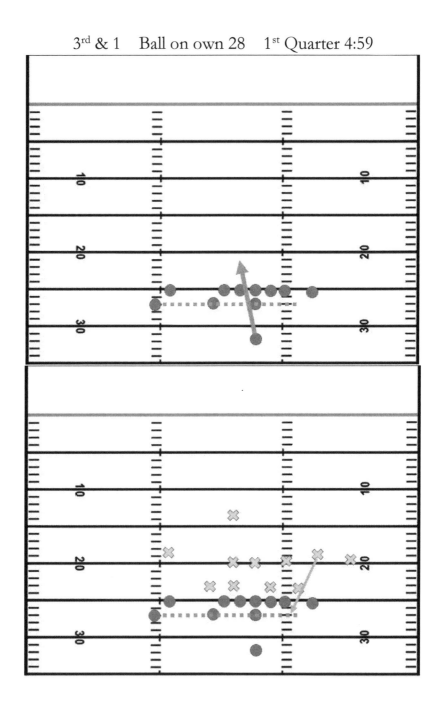

With a third and one on tap, the Saints run a fullback dive play.

The Saints send a tight end in motion to create an extra gap on their right. The Buccaneers react by rolling down a safety to account for the gap.

The Saints get a strong double team on the 1 technique, and the fullback falls into the filling linebacker just in time to pick up the first down.

3rd & 9   Ball on own 9   2nd Quarter 12:15

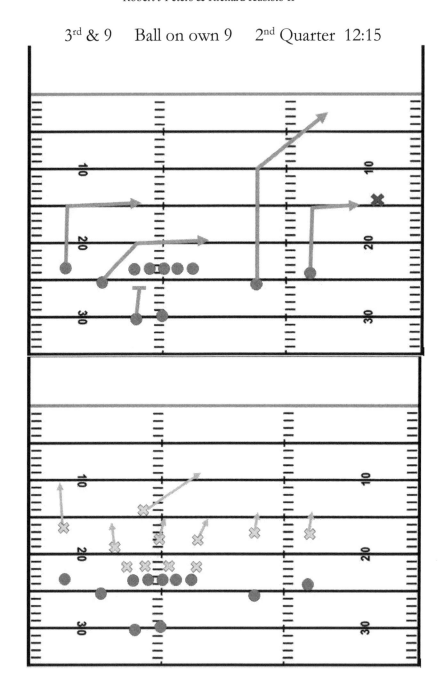

Progression Read:

1. 10 Yard Out
2. Corner Route
3. Drag
4. Dig

The Saints snap the ball quickly on this third and long deep in their own territory. They call a long version of the smash concept on the front side, and the drive concept on the back side. The "smash long" concept gives the Saints an extra option past the first down marker, a nice adjustment given the down and distance.

The Buccaneers aggressively match the patterns on the front side. Brees throws the 10 yard out on rhythm, and the corner breaks the play up, forcing a fourth down.

3rd & 1   Ball on Tampa Bay 44   2nd Quarter 7:51

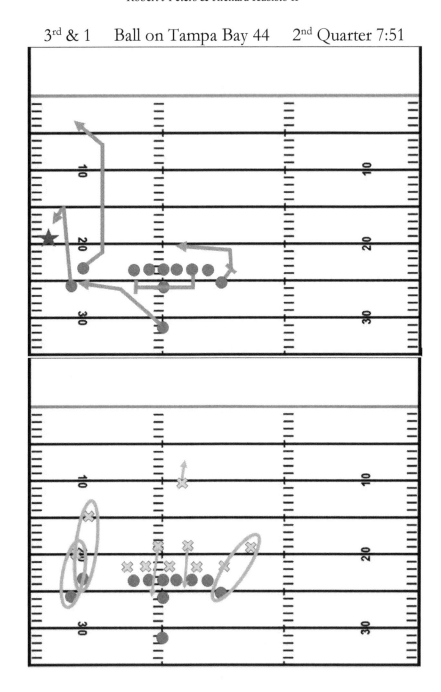

Progression Read:

1. Alert: Corner Route
2. 10 Yard Curl
3. RB Flat
4. TE Chip-Release Drag

The Saints pull a guard and take a shot down field on this third and short. The curl concept they use has been a staple of the west coast offense for years. The outside stem and initial break of the curl route is meant to give the receiver inside leverage to come back to the quarterback.

The Buccaneers play man coverage with a free safety to help over the top. They play inside – out on the two receiver stack.

The corner route runner does a fantastic job of turning his man's hips and beating him deep. Great teaching tape.

The defense jumps offside, but the penalty is declined as Brees hits the curl route on time to pick up a first down.

3ʳᵈ & 3   Ball on Tampa Bay 24   2ⁿᵈ Quarter 6:54

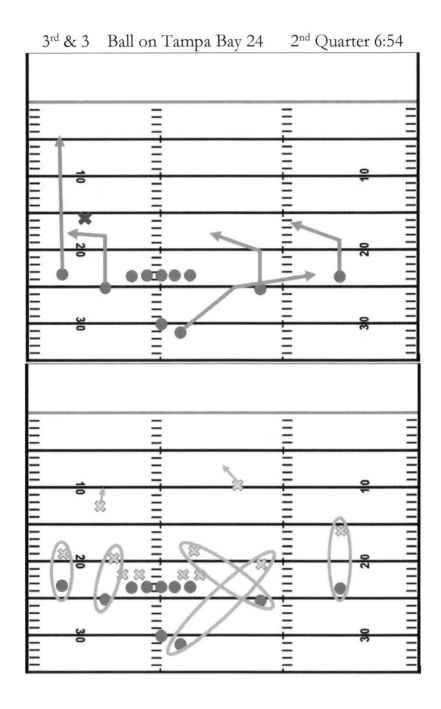

The Saints call a man pick concept on the right. The slot will run into the inside linebacker, trying to free up the running back to get leverage for his flat route.

The Buccaneers play an aggressive cover 4 pattern match. The strong side linebacker and middle linebacker do a nice job of swapping routes. The strong side linebacker triggers hard on the flat route once he sees his man go inside.

Brees recognizes the zone shell, and likes the leverage he sees with his flat route on the left side. The pass is slightly in front of the receiver, who probably could have mad the catch anyways. The incomplete pass brings up fourth down.

3rd & 11 Ball on Tampa Bay 20 Quarter 2 :27

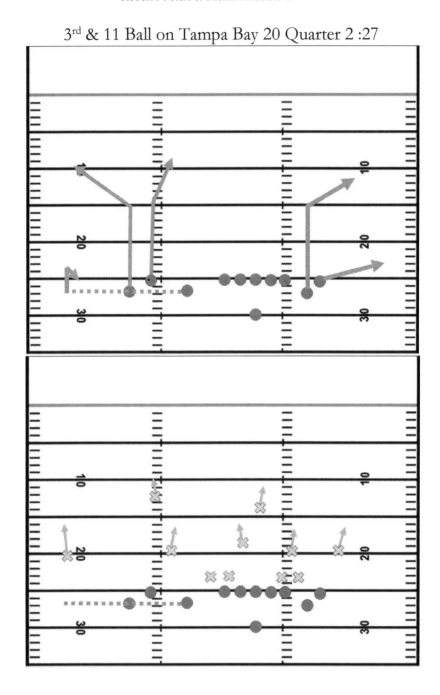

Coverage Read:

1. Vs single high safety: Throw a hitch route
2. Vs two high safeties: throw away from the rotation. The concept gives the quarterback three verticals on two deep safeties. If the corners bail, throw the hitch.

The Saints call a smash split on a third and long in the red zone. The play call works well against two high safeties, which is a common defensive shell for a third and long.

The Buccaneers play a soft cover two. The corners drop off of the hitch routes to give a reasonable amount of help on the corner routes. The safety to the wide side of the field puts himself in the perfect position to defend both vertical routes at their break points. He has the proper depth and hip alignment.

These factors cause the quarterback to hold the ball and scramble for a couple of yards. The great coverage brings up a fourth down.

3rd & 4   Ball on Tampa Bay 11   3rd Quarter 6:24

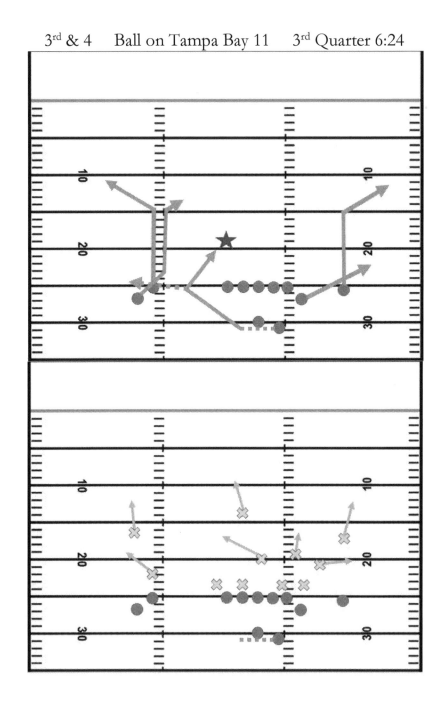

The Saints call this third down play with the memory of the last third down fresh in their heads. The base concept of the play stays the same as the play on the previous page. The Saints use a slight twist to take advantage of the way the Buccaneers matched the routes. The Buccaneers matched the vertical split route on the previous page by walling him off with their inside linebacker.

The back out of the backfield will run an angle route. This route takes advantage of a middle linebacker walling off of a vertical down the middle of the field against two high safeties.

The Buccaneers play an aggressive cover 4 on this third down, and use the same principles to wall off the post route on the left.

The Saints take full advantage of this, and score a touchdown on an outstanding play call.

3rd & 16   Ball on Tampa Bay 24   4th Quarter 13:20

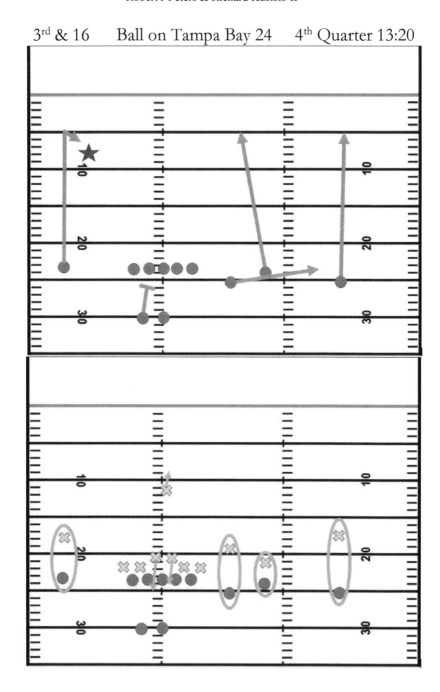

Progression Read:

1. Stalk & go from the #2 on the right
2. Deep curl from #1 on left

The Saints call a double move concept on this third down. The receivers on the trips side of the field will simulate a flat screen. The #2 receiver will sell a stalk block, and run up the seam.

The play works perfectly. The stalk & go from the #2 receiver sells the man to man defender, and he breaks free.

For some reason, Brees gets off this receiver before he breaks open. He steps up in the pocket, and resets his feet to the deep curl route.

The play times up perfectly, and Brees hits the deep curl right on time to pick up the first down.

3rd and Goal   Ball on Tampa Bay 3   4th Quarter 12:00

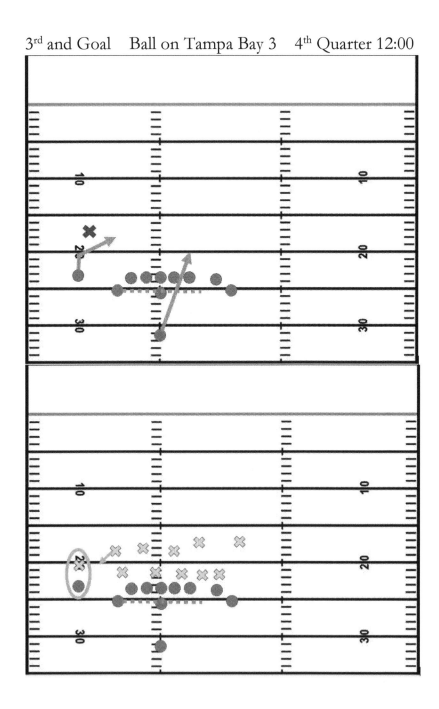

Coverage Read: "RPO": QB throws slant if he has enough space and inside leverage. If not, hand the ball off.

The Saints call a dive play to the right, with a built in slant route to the single receiver.

The Buccaneers trap the Saints on this third down, and almost shift the tide of the game with a pick six. The safety times up the snap count perfectly, and sprints to the slant window. The ball gets knocked down, and almost intercepted. The incompletion brings up a fourth down.

3rd & 10   Ball on own 35   4th Quarter 4:50

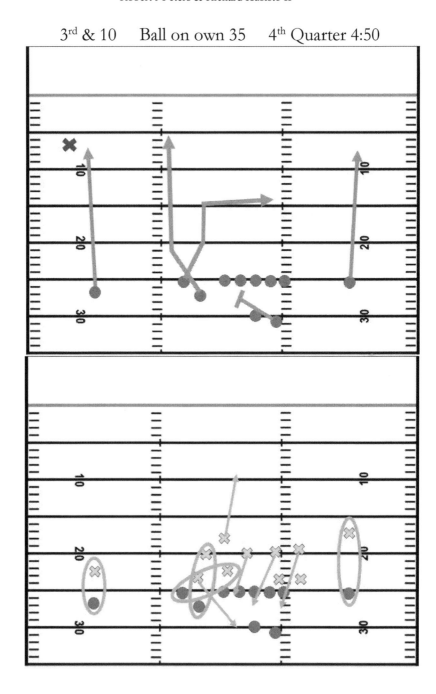

Coverage Read

1. Vs single high safety: throw the slot seam away from the rotation.
2. Vs two high safeties: pick a side and throw one of the verticals away from that safety.

The Saints call their four vertical concept out of a compressed trips formation, with the two slot receivers tight to the left tackle. The play is meant to look like their "H Post" concept.

The Buccaneers come out in a press man, cover zero pressure look. When the ball is snapped, the safety bails to help in the deep middle of the field.

The Saints get the one on one matchups they were hoping for, but not the leverage. After the disguise, the defenders on the seam routes play with a cushion, and meet the receiver at their landmarks.

Brees sees a one on one on the outside, and takes the chance on the fade to the wide side of the field. the throw is slightly behind the intended target, forcing a fourth down.

3rd & 1   Ball on Tampa Bay 36   4th Quarter 1:51

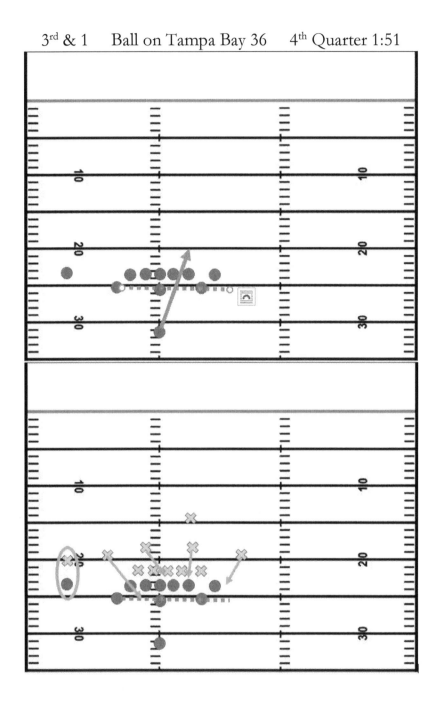

The Saints are trying to put the Buccaneers away with this drive. With a one possession lead late in the fourth quarter, converting first downs wins you football games.

The Saints call their dive play to the right. The offensive line will block the gap to their left, allowing the three tight ends to create the wedge needed for the first down.

The Saints wash down all of the down lineman for the Buccaneers. They get the three tight ends in position for their blocks. The back side linebacker does not get blocked, and meets the back in the hole. With a slight jump cut, the running back gets past this defender and picks up the first down.

Robert J Peters & Richard Kusisto II

Week 17 at Atlanta

3rd & 11   Ball on own 24   1st Quarter 14:25

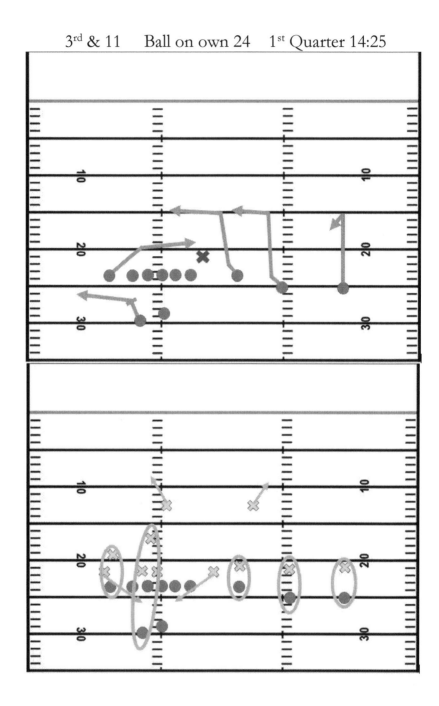

Progression Read:

1. #3 Dig
2. #2 Dig
3. Shallow Cross

The Saints use this four vertical variation on third down. Brees reads the safety to the short side of the field first. With the safety staying on the hash, Brees moves on from the #3 on the dig, to the #2 dig route, trying to get behind the middle linebacker.

As Brees gets off of the dig from the #2 receiver, he escapes the pocket and throws the drag route. The Falcons tight man coverage blankets the drag route, and forces a punt on fourth down.

3rd & 1   Ball on own 34   1st Quarter 10:43

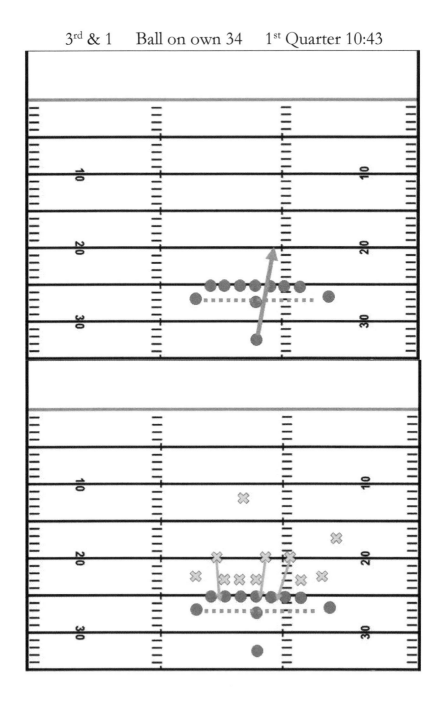

The Saints run a dive play, often referred to as "Duo" or Double" on third and short. This play gives the offense a double team block on the play side 1 technique.

The Saints get a good push from the center and right guard. The right tackle gets a nice block on the inside linebacker, and allows the running back to pick up the first down before an outside linebacker makes the tackle.

3rd & 11   Ball on own 35   1st Quarter 8:49

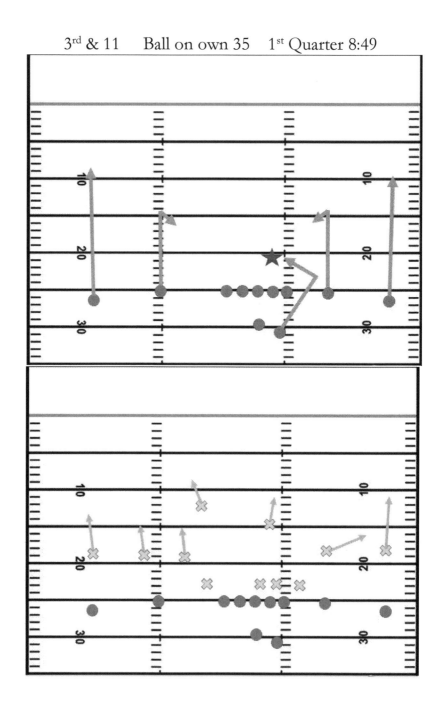

Coverage Read:

1. Vs single high safeties: Key slot receiver off of the rotation of the safeties.
2. Vs two high safeties: Key the running back in a 1 on 1 vs linebacker.

The Saints call four verticals, with route conversions. The slots hitch up at ten yards when they determine they can't get vertical separation.

The Falcons play a conservative cover three on this third and long. The underneath defenders are playing the first down line, and eventually match the vertical stems after 8 yards.

With the flat defender expanding to get width, the safety defending the hook zone breaks on the hitch route from the slot to the right. Brees hits his running back in the void left by the safety on time, which allows the Saints to pick up the first down.

3rd & 2   Ball on Atlanta 31   1st Quarter 6:48

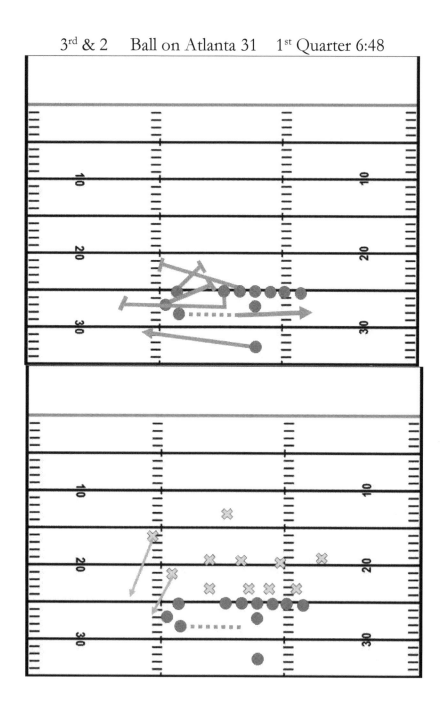

The Saints fake a jet sweep, and call a toss play on this third and short. The defensive end to the play side gets up the field quickly, which pushes the tackle to get more depth. The defensive end is blocked by the slot receiver, and washed down the line of scrimmage.

The left tackle is unable to block the corner, who spills inside to tackle the running back. The running back could have helped his tackle out by staying outside, instead of cutting inside as quickly as he did. The running back is tackled short of the first down.

3rd & 1   Ball on Atlanta 1   1st Quarter 4:01

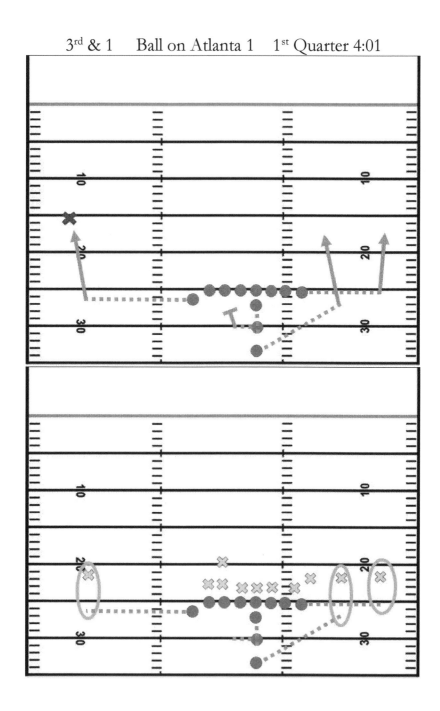

The Saints shift out of a 32 personnel goal line formation, to get their tight ends matched up on the outside with smaller or slower defenders.

The Saints call fades to their outside receivers, and the quarterback determines pre-snap that he likes the matchup to his left. The Falcons shift over a smaller safety to guard the larger tight end, a matchup friendly to the offense.

The play is initially called a touchdown, but after review is changed to an incompletion.

3rd & 8   Ball on own 27   2nd Quarter 12:50

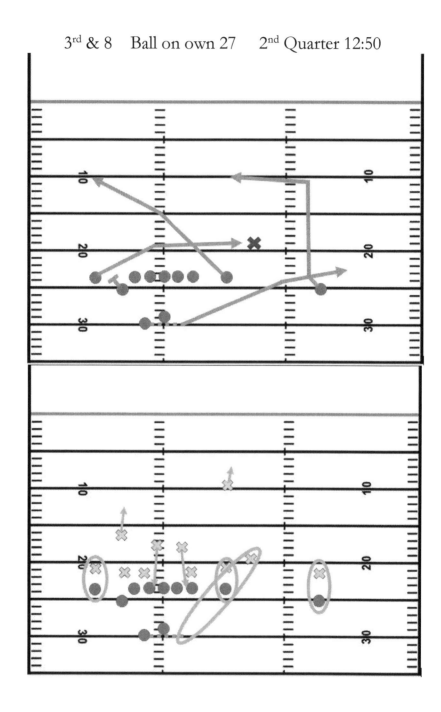

Progression Read:

1. RB Flat
2. Shallow Drag from #1 on left
3. Deep Cross from #2 on right
4. Dig

The Saints shift the running back to identify man coverage. the defensive end changes sides of the formation as the back shifts. The play the Saints have called gives the quarterback a nice progression against man coverage as well as single safety zone coverages. The flat and shallow have the ability to occupy the two underneath defenders on the right, opening up a nice window for the dig route.

The Falcons play man coverage, and bring a fifth rusher. The Saints have enough bodies to protect their quarterback, but they lose the one on one matchup with their right guard.

Brees gets forced to throw the ball away, which brings up a fourth down.

3rd & 9   Ball on own 26   2nd Quarter 4:28

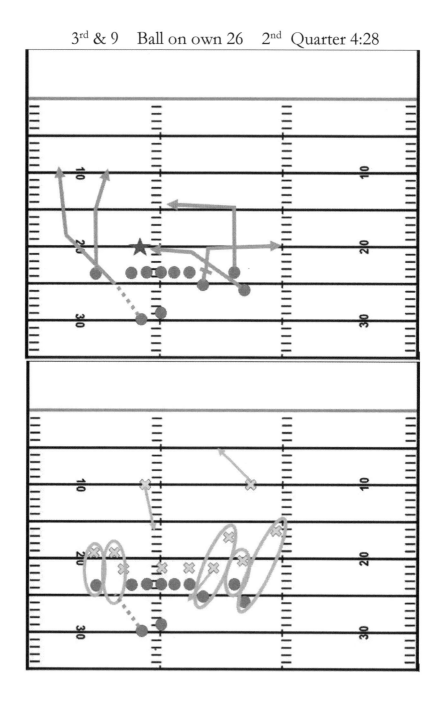

Progression Read:

1. Alert: Post
2. Wheel
3. Drag
4. Dig
5. RB Check Down

The Saints call a two man drive concept on this third down. On the front side they will typically run a 10 yard out with the slot and a clear out from the widest receiver. This time they pair the drive concept with a wheel route from the running back who is aligned in the slot.

The Falcons call a cover 1 cross bracket. This coverage allows the robber to match any crossing routes he sees coming to his side. This ends up being the perfect call to bait the QB into throwing the drag route.

Brees sees the Falcons match the wheel and post on his front side, which opens up a window for the drag route entering his vision. He does not see the robbing safety come down. The safety makes the tackle immediately, and brings up fourth down.

3rd & 17   Ball on own 37   3rd Quarter 11:09

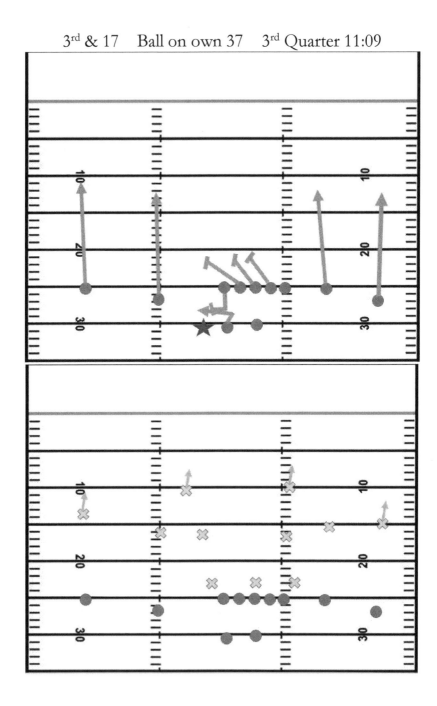

With a third and forever, the Saints call a screen to the running back. The Falcons bring a three man rush, so the quarterback has a clean window to get the ball to his back.

The Saints' offensive line does a nice job of getting downfield and setting up their blocks. With the Falcons playing a prevent style coverage, they have more than enough bodies to make the play.

The center and guard lose sight of the nickel for a second, allowing him to cut under the block. He tackles the running back shy of the first down, forcing the Saints to punt.

3rd & 12   Ball on own 23 3rd Quarter 4:43

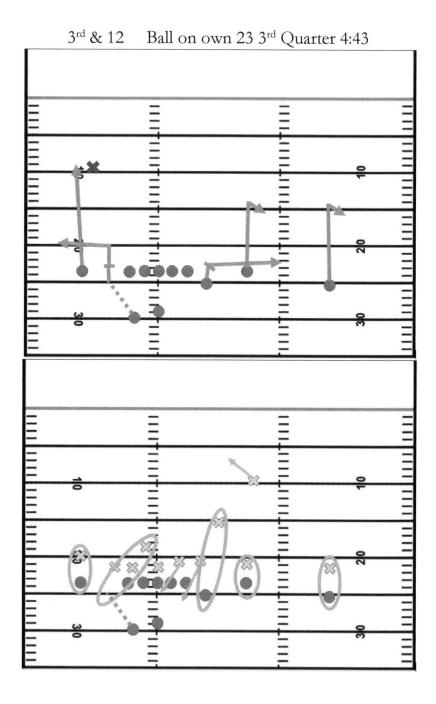

Progression Read:

1. Inside Curl
2. Outside Curl
3. Flat

The Saints call one of their go – to empty plays, the "Hank" concept. At the line of scrimmage before the ball is snapped, Brees signals a fade route to the receiver on the left. The corner is lined up pressing him, with inside leverage. The curl route would be difficult to overcome this positioning, so Brees adjusted the play. This changes his progression, as he is eyeing the big play in this one on one matchup.

The corner plays with perfect position, and puts himself in a great place to defend the fade route.

The pass is broken up and falls incomplete.

3rd & 10   Ball on own 22   4th Quarter 14:02

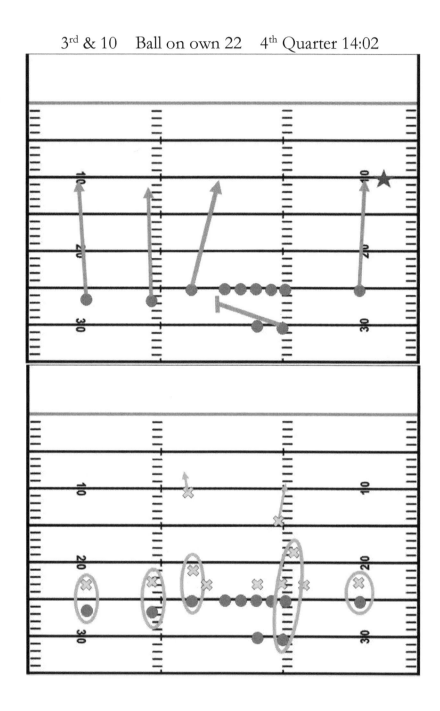

Coverage Read

1. Vs Single High Safety: Key slot receivers, throw opposite safety rotation
2. Vs Two High Safeties: Read safety to single receiver side for 1 on 1, then #3 receiver to #2 receiver on trips side.

The Saints call four verticals on this third and long. The Falcons come out playing man under, two deep. This coverage is typically sound against four verticals.

The two safeties are both squeezing the middle of the field tightly. As Brees eyes the safety to the short side of the field, he sees no help for the corner matched up one on one with his single receiver to the short side of the field.

The Saints convert on a great throw and catch to pick up the first down.

3rd & 13   Ball on Atlanta 49   4th Quarter 8:30

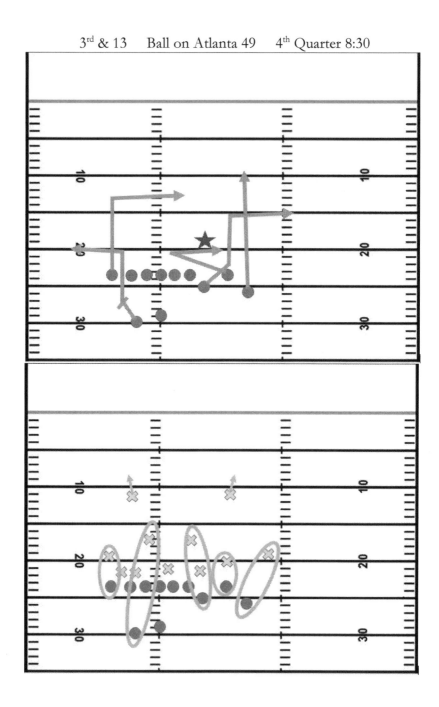

Progression Read:

1. 10 Yard Out
2. Whip
3. Dig
4. RB Check Down

This play call is the most effective, and most creative in this game for the Saints. They call a version of the flood concept, that is meant to look like the drive concept that they've used throughout the season (page xx).

The Falcons play man coverage, once again. They also have two high safeties over the top. The two high safeties allow the underneath defenders to play more aggressively, as they have a safety blanket behind them.

The whip route pushes hard to the inside, and breaks extremely late. The route breaks over the center. This late break forces the man defender to commit to defending the drag. The Whip route gains the outside leverage and picks up a big gain and first down.

The effort from the other receiver to recover the fumble at the end of this play is great teaching tape to show players the importance of never quitting on a play.

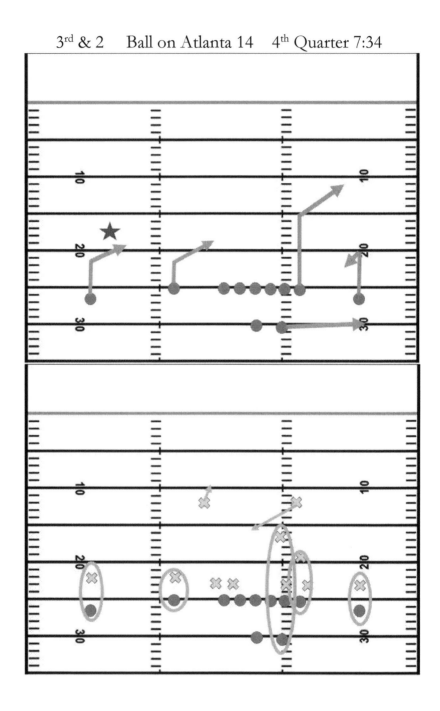

3rd & 2   Ball on Atlanta 14   4th Quarter 7:34

Coverage Read:

4. Vs single high safety: Read Snag concept on the right (flat – spot)
5. Vs two high safeties: read slants on left (inside – out)
6. Vs man: pick matchups and leverage that favor the offense

With the Falcons playing a heavy dose of man coverage, Brees keys his matchups and leverage that he likes on this third and short.

With a ton of space to the wide side of the field, he hits the outside slant route to pick up the first down. The accuracy displayed on this throw is tremendous. Brees throws the ball to the back hip of the receiver, to keep in away from the defender.

3rd & 1   Ball on Atlanta 1   4th Quarter 2:50

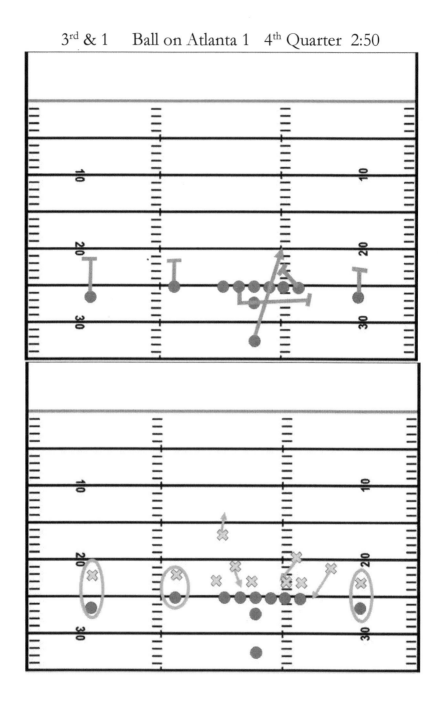

With third and goal from the one, The Saints call a long trap concept to the tight end side. The play looks like power initially, but the tight end blocks down, and chips up to the linebacker. . The pulling guard has his eyes set on the trap block on the defensive end outside of the tight end.

The running back jumps over the pile and scores a touchdown.

3rd & 5   Ball on own 48   4th Quarter 2:25

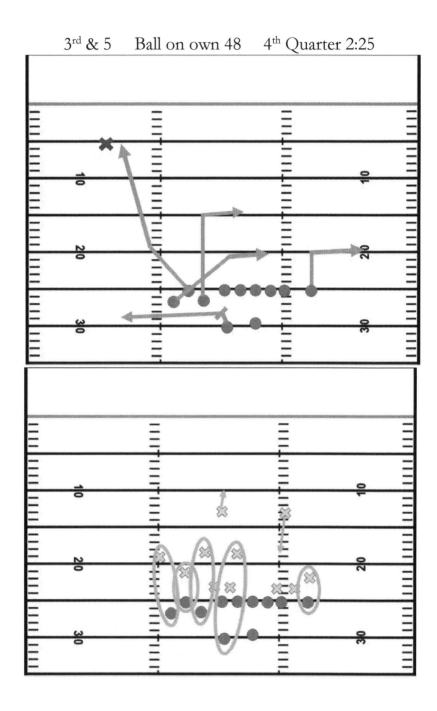

Progression Read:

1. Alert Fade
2. Corner Route
3. Drag
4. Dig
5. RB Check Down

The Saints call their drive concept out of the bunch formation, hoping to get some rubs against man coverage. The Falcons come out with the perfect defensive call, a cover 1 cross bracket.

The cross bracket helps tremendously in this case. The robbing safety is allowed to come down on the drag route, which allows the man defender on the drag to become the new robber. The new robber sits in the dig window. This play is a great clip on how to play sound man coverage.

None of these details matter on this particular play, as Brees sees the matchup on his slot fade route, and determines that is where he is going with the ball pre-snap.

The ball is well-thrown, but the defender is in perfect position and the pass falls incomplete.

3rd & 1   Ball on Atlanta 30   4th Quarter 1:39

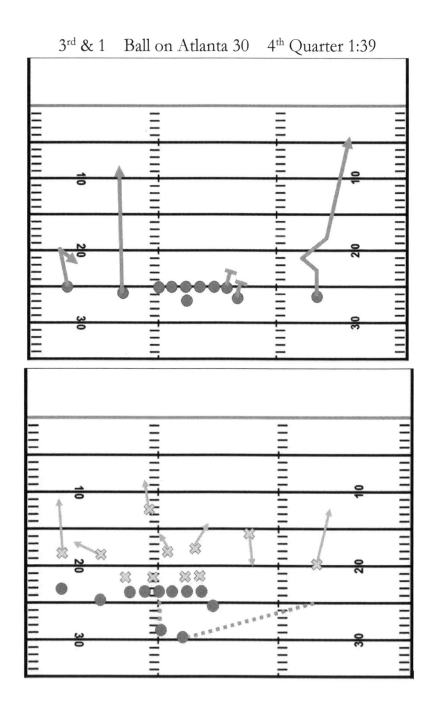

Progression Read:

1. Slant n Go (Sluggo)
2. Seam
3. Hitch

The Saints call an old west coast staple, "Sluggo Seam". This concept is best against a single high safety, exactly what the Falcons give them. If the Sluggo is covered, the seam should be open. The safety will have moved to the Sluggo side because of the quarterback's eyes, opening up the window for the seam.

The corner plays off coverage on the Sluggo, forcing Brees to reset his feet to the backside seam route. This route opens up and Brees pulls the trigger.

The ball flutters and falls incomplete.

3ʳᵈ & 5   Ball on Atlanta 12   4ᵗʰ Quarter 1:01

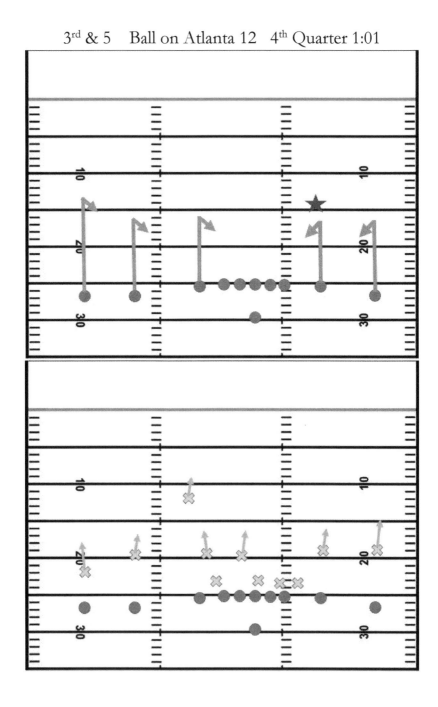

With the time winding down in a two possession game, the Saints call an all hitch concept out of empty. The Falcons play a conservative zone in order to prevent the easy touchdown.

Brees finds the largest cushion, and hits the hitch route to his right to pick up the first down.

Robert J Peters & Richard Kusisto II

ABOUT THE AUTHORS

Bobby currently coaches at Marmion Academy, in Aurora Illinois. You can find more of his work at:

www.theofficialpetersreport.blogspot.com

Email: bpeters1212@gmail.com

Books on Amazon

The Melting Pot: How to Acclimate Old NFL Concepts into Your High School or College Offense

Richard currently coaches at Grand Forks Central High in Grand Forks, North Dakota.